Unconditional Happiness:

My Life Experience To Self-Realization

(Treasure Book for My Children)

Rameen Zereh

Contents

Introduction 1

Chapter 1   The Mirage of Identity 12

Chapter 2   Truth Beyond Illusion 16

Chapter 3   Unmasking the True Self 23

Chapter 4   The Journey Within 34

Chapter 5   Purpose Beyond the Self 44

Chapter 6   Emerging from Shadows 54

Chapter 7   Nothing Like the Present 63

Chapter 8   The Blueprint of Manifestation 73

Chapter 9   The Layers of Existence 87

Chapter 10   Cosmic Order and Metaphysical Truths 100

Chapter 11   The Quest for Peace Within 112

Chapter 12   Living Between Two Identities 121

Chapter 13   The Awakening of the True Self 139

Chapter 14   The Foundation of Religion, Spirituality, and the Divine 152

Conclusion 165

References 177

Introduction

Strong and ambitious, I stepped out of high school as a fresh graduate, with the world before me, the earth beneath me, and the sky as my only limit. Looking back, I now realize it marked the beginning of my journey toward self-realization. I was brimming with dreams, ambitions, pride, and hope—yet my aspirations were fragile, built on a shaky foundation of fears and desires. I feared being insignificant, worthless, and trapped in scarcity, as I had grown up with little—no house, no riches, no secure future, not even a country to call my own.

I know what it feels like to be displaced, homeless, and forced to leave behind everything familiar and cherished. I have experienced the blow to my pride when my family had to depend on social services as immigrants. I clung to the false belief that material comforts and external achievements could bring me happiness. I was too young and naïve to understand that happiness doesn't come from the outside—that my essence is unconditional happiness, untouched by external circumstances.

At the time, I aspired to become an aeronautic engineer at NASA. I planned to earn a bachelor's degree in science from San Jose State University, begin my dream career, and pursue further education while working. I imagined that my hard work would lead to a high income, and with that, I could live a happy life. I see now how misguided that belief was. Little did I know the universe had different plans for me.

I learned late in life that happiness is not something to be sought in the external world. It is an intrinsic part of yourself, accessible only by looking within. This understanding is why I always remind my children to embrace unconditional happiness, regardless of their circumstances. The essence of the universe and the supreme power is absolute love and boundless joy. Our True Self is inherently full of love and happiness. Though discovering this inner truth may take time, the journey is inevitable, and I am here to guide you through it.

What Does This Book Offer?

This is not just another spirituality book, nor is it simply the autobiography of an old man. I invite readers to join me on a journey—

my journey to discovering my Truth—in the hope that it will inspire my children and others to uncover their own Truth. This book serves as both a father's legacy and a heartfelt guide for my two beloved sons.

Realizing my Truth brought me freedom from the delusions of the mind and the suffering they create. It is a blessing that has transformed every aspect of my life in unimaginable ways, and it is a gift I wish to share with everyone, especially with my own family.

The ideas and reflections I have shared in this book may provoke criticism, but to truly grasp the message within, it is essential to approach it with an open mind—one that is flexible and willing to embrace change.

"The measure of intelligence is the ability to change."

– Albert Einstein.

An open mind, willing to embrace challenging beliefs and ideas, becomes the foundation for meaningful change—a change that offers a fresh perspective and the opportunity to embark on a journey of self-realization. Self-realization does not depend on intelligence or IQ; it relies on emotional intelligence (EQ). Awareness and spirituality are understood through the heart, not the mind. While the mind is rational and bound by logic, the heart experiences spirituality through emotions and feelings that lead to deeper self-awareness.

A limited mind cannot fully comprehend or articulate the infinite. To truly grow, one must release the shackles that hinder spiritual exploration. These shackles can take many forms—your sense of identity, inherited beliefs, upbringing, relationships, education, or even a lack of it. Perhaps you were taught to believe in only the material world, with nothing beyond it, or that your physical self and its immediate needs were all that mattered. Such constraints prevent you from discovering the boundless realm of spirituality. To move forward, you must first free yourself from these limitations.

I share this with the utmost respect and without intent to criticize anyone. I recognize that not everyone can easily break free from the ties that bind them. My aim is simply to speak my Truth openly, with sincerity, for those who are ready to receive it. A true learner remains unoffended and a seeker of Truth welcomes diverse perspectives.

The world is a masterpiece, and like any work of art, it inspires a multitude of interpretations. Similarly, though this book shares "my Truth," it leaves space for the understanding that you have your own Truth as well. Two people can witness the same phenomenon yet derive distinct realizations, perceptions, and interpretations—all equally valid. That is the beauty of Truth—it is multifaceted and personal.

My goal is not to change anyone, but to honor my Truth by sharing it with my boys and my readers. This book reflects the beauty I have discovered in my journey, and I hope it inspires others to embrace their own path. Above all, I hope my readers will grasp the importance of approaching life—and this book—with an open mind, for such openness is essential to this journey.

"Having a mind that is open to everything and attached to nothing is an evolving and unlimited mind."

– Dr. Wayne Dyer

What Can You Take Away from This Book?

Being a college dropout, dyslexic, and an immigrant with English as my second language, I have faced unique challenges in expressing myself. Yet, I will do my best to articulate the realization of my Truth—a Truth that has granted me the freedom to simply be, observing the dance of life from a detached perspective, free from judgment or personal involvement.

All humans possess the ability and the right to discover their Truth. This Truth liberates us from the bonds of suffering, enabling a life unburdened and effortless, even within this world. This book attempts to conceptualize, guide, and describe the realization of my Truth—the nameless, shapeless, formless, limitless, and timeless essence. While fully capturing such a profound experience is impossible, I aim to provide a glimpse of its transformative power.

A Little About Me

My journey began in the heart of Afghanistan, where I was born and raised as a proud Afghan Muslim. My father worked for the United Nations in Afghanistan, but in 1984, when I turned 12, our lives were forever altered. The Soviet occupation had plunged Kabul into chaos, creating a dangerous and unpredictable environment. Each day, young boys were forcibly recruited into the Afghan Army. I lived a real-life game of hide-and-seek, avoiding lineups where soldiers chose men and boys—some as young as 14—based on whether they had facial hair. These boys were sent to war zones with minimal training, facing a survival rate of less than 30%.

The constant threat of being drafted loomed large, and my parents were determined to protect me. They knew enlisting in the army during the Soviet occupation was akin to a death sentence. Despite their deep patriotism, they made the heart-wrenching decision to flee Afghanistan. Leaving our beloved country was an act of survival, the only way to ensure our safety and future.

Daily life in Kabul during the Soviet occupation was fraught with fear and uncertainty. Citizens faced constant danger, unsure whether they would return home after work or school. The city became a battleground as freedom fighters, known as Mujahideen, targeted Soviet forces, their Afghan allies, and civilians caught in the crossfire. Bombings of public places like movie theaters and buses made everyday life perilous.

Amid this turmoil, my father, who had previously been an exchange student in America and lived with an American family, the Fiskes, saw an opportunity for safety. The Fiskes, gracious and compassionate, sponsored our family's immigration to the United States. This act of kindness allowed us to escape the chaos of Kabul and begin a new chapter in Marysville, California.

At that time, we were completely lost. The Fiskes family became our guiding light, helping us transition into a new life. As newly arrived refugees, we had no idea where to begin. Their financial support and unwavering kindness made us feel welcome from the moment we arrived. Although we soon moved into our own home nearby, their support remained a crucial foundation during our early days in the United States.

Starting over in a new country was daunting. We had no home, no future, and no hope. I felt lost, directionless, and consumed by anxiety. Just a few years after our arrival, tragedy struck—my father passed away. At only 20 years old, I was suddenly thrust into the role of breadwinner for a family of six. Confused and overwhelmed, I had to juggle working, managing the family business, and pursuing my university studies.

My father had established a small electronics store at a flea market, selling toasters and other small appliances. When he passed away in 1993, I inherited this modest business. Despite my inexperience, I dedicated every ounce of effort to making it succeed. Initially, the store earned a modest fifty thousand dollars a year—just enough to keep us afloat. It offered a sliver of hope and stability, though far from the security we needed.

Balancing the demands of running the business and maintaining my academic responsibilities proved to be too much. The weight of it all forced me to make a difficult decision—I left school to focus entirely on supporting my family and growing the business. There were countless sleepless nights, moments of doubt, and times when I questioned whether I could endure the pressure. Yet, through it all, I found strength in surrendering to God's will. Living day by day, I discovered a natural flow to life that carried me forward, even when I felt I had no strength left to give.

Through relentless dedication and hard work, I began to see the fruits of my labor. The business grew steadily, and eventually, annual sales soared past a million dollars. This success brought us the comfort and stability we had once only dreamed of. My journey was fraught with challenges, but it also became a testament to the resilience of the human spirit and the power of unwavering faith.

I owe much of my success to the unwavering emotional support of my mother and grandmother. Their love, strength, and wisdom were the bedrock upon which I built my determination and perseverance. Their belief in me gave me the courage to keep moving forward, even in the face of overwhelming adversity.

My mother epitomized sacrifice and dedication, profoundly shaping the trajectory of our family's journey and business success. After my father's passing, she devoted herself entirely to her children, ensuring we had the support and guidance needed to thrive. Together with my grandmother, she became an unwavering pillar of strength, providing stability and nurturing my siblings with love and resilience.

During those challenging years, we faced countless obstacles, but my mother's determination never wavered. She worked tirelessly, often setting aside her own needs to prioritize our family's well-being. Her sacrifices were immense—from long hours of labor to sleepless nights spent worrying about our future. Her perseverance and commitment were instrumental in guiding us through those difficult times until business opportunities allowed us to grow and flourish.

Her strength and selflessness became a beacon of hope for our family and an enduring source of inspiration for my siblings and me. My mother's legacy of love and dedication is deeply etched in our hearts, a reminder of the power of unwavering commitment and the profound impact it can have on our lives. She is, without a doubt, the cornerstone of our success and the embodiment of a devoted, loving mother.

After fifteen years of compounded business growth, the Great Recession of 2008 struck like a bolt of lightning, and my once-thriving business began to unravel. The anxiety and helplessness I felt during this time were overwhelming. Desperate for reprieve, I placed my trust in my business partner—a person I had mentored since he was a teenager. Over the years, I had taught him everything about the business, nurturing his skills and watching him grow. To me, he was not just a partner but a protégé, someone I believed shared my values and commitment to our mutual success.

In my desperation, I decided to step back, hoping that a break would help me regain my strength and clarity. Entrusting him with the reins of the business, I believed he would manage it with the same care and dedication I had. I placed my faith in him, trusting that he would reciprocate the hard work and loyalty I had shown him. However, his true intentions soon became clear. Rather than uphold our shared vision, he sought only his own gain. This betrayal was devastating. My partner, whom I had supported and trusted, seized everything—my business, my savings, and my properties—leaving me in complete ruin.

The financial devastation was staggering. Everything I had worked so hard to build for my family—the stability and security we relied on—was gone. Yet, the emotional toll was even greater. The betrayal felt like a deep personal wound, inflicted by someone I had considered family. Losing trust in someone so close, and grappling with the feelings of manipulation and deceit, left me reeling. I was not only facing financial ruin but also struggling to process the profound sense of betrayal and the shattering of my faith in people.

This period of my life was marked by intense emotional turmoil. I felt broken in every conceivable way—financially, emotionally, and spiritually.

It was as though the ground beneath me had vanished, leaving me to navigate an overwhelming darkness. Every day was a struggle to survive, to endure, and to find a way forward through the pain and disillusionment that had engulfed my life.

Despite these hardships, this period became a time of deep introspection and eventual transformation. The betrayal forced me to confront my vulnerabilities and reevaluate the illusions I held about trust and loyalty. Through the anguish, I began to discover the importance of inner strength and resilience. Slowly, I learned to surrender my burdens to a higher power, finding solace in the realization that even in the darkest times, there is room for growth and renewal. This excruciating experience ultimately led me to a deeper understanding of myself and the world around me.

The following years were among the darkest I had ever known, marked by poverty, despair, and an ongoing battle against a victim mentality. For years, I faced unemployment, a lack of income, and the paralyzing fear of an uncertain future. I felt utterly broken—financially, emotionally, and spiritually. Yet, in the depths of this darkness, a subtle shift began to take shape. I started to question everything I thought I knew about myself and the structures that had defined my identity.

Through the practice of mindfulness and awareness, I gained a new perspective. I learned to observe my pain without becoming it, to witness my thoughts without letting them control me. This transformative shift made me realize that my hardships were not punishments but opportunities for growth. Forgiveness became a powerful tool on this journey. I found the strength to forgive my former partner—not for his sake, but for my own. Releasing anger and resentment allowed me to reclaim my power and move forward.

My journey through the recession and betrayal became a path of self-discovery and empowerment, transforming adversity into a steppingstone toward a deeper and more enlightened existence.

This challenging period was an essential aspect of my journey. It was a nightmare to endure, yet, like nightmares that jolt us awake, these harsh times forced me to awaken from the illusions of my mind. Smooth sailing in life only serves to perpetuate the illusion; it is in hardship that true awakening begins.

During those smooth sails, I built a false identity—Rameen Zereh. I thought I was not enough, always feeling a hole in my heart, a longing, an emptiness, and an insatiable thirst for something I could not name. I misidentified myself with my mind's illusions—its thoughts, feelings, emotions, perceptions, ego, and identity.

The pain, both physical and emotional, was overwhelming. I suffered from stomach ulcers, chest pain, high blood pressure, asthma, and anxiety. Every day brought a new episode of the same old suffering. I feared dying in the middle of the night, often staying awake for days because I was terrified that if I slept, I might never wake up again.

Worry consumed me—worry about losing my business, paying bills, and depleting my life savings. I lived on an emotional roller coaster, and it got so bad that I wanted my suffering to end. Sadness came in waves, leaving me feeling like I was drowning, tossed and thrashed against the rocks. I sought escape in alcohol, overeating, oversleeping, gambling, and shopping, trying anything to numb the pain temporarily.

I would disappear for days, gambling in Lake Tahoe or Las Vegas, sometimes for 72 hours straight, only to return home to my poor wife, who had no idea where I had been. It was a disappointing time in my life, and I apologize to her daily for my neglect. I lost myself in fleeting worldly pleasures, only to pay the price with months of guilt, shame, and worthlessness.

Through this, I learned that no amount of worldly power, wealth, or pleasure could fill the void within me. Temporary fixes only quenched the thirst momentarily, but the emptiness always returned, stronger than before.

By my early 40s, while still misidentifying with my body, mind, and ego, I began to question life's purpose and meaning. Though I was born into Islam, I followed it as a birthright rather than as a practicing believer. Religion was not a part of my life—only suffering was, and it brought endless questions.

What is this suffering? Why is nothing ever enough? Why does happiness come and go but never stay? Do material things hold the key to happiness, or is true happiness found within? Who or what am I?

To find the answers, I had to look inward, quiet my mind, and connect with my source. This reflection revealed the stark difference between religion and spirituality. While religion involves following a prophet's life and a holy book's rules, spirituality demands waking up from the societal and religious constructs imposed on us. Spirituality is like tasting honey for oneself, while religion is hearing someone else describe its taste.

At the time, neither religion nor spirituality was part of my life—only suffering and the search for answers. Now, having seen the bigger picture, I am free from the pendulum of judgment. I can look back at my naïve self without scorn, marveling at the transformation. To offer a metaphor, though it may not fully capture the truth: I was like Superman all along, yet I always chose to live as Clark Kent.

The journey was painful and relentless, but it was entirely worth it for the liberation from my enslaved identity and mind. Externally, little has changed—my body still experiences pain, discomfort, impatience, anger, and jealousy. Yet, since discovering my true self, I no longer react to these bodily and mental experiences. Instead, I maintain a sense of distance, acting as a non-judgmental, unbiased witness to all that unfolds.

I have become an actor in my reality, rather than a reactor. My true self remains unchanging and constant, allowing me to see every person and circumstance as a test. This perspective helps me avoid reacting impulsively to situations or others' behaviors. There are moments when my ego tries to emerge, eager to defend my mind-created identity, but my awareness keeps it in check.

With this newfound awareness, I stay tranquil and at peace. My mind no longer has the power to drag me through the roller coaster of thoughts, emotions, and feelings. Instead, my mind, body, ego, and personality have become tools—functions that serve me rather than control me.

I still engage in life's activities. I work, go to movies and restaurants, enjoy vacations, attend clubs and parties, and maintain relationships. I continue to be a father, brother, son, and husband. However, I now approach these roles from a place of detachment, as a mindful and unchanging witness. As I navigate my day, shifting from one role to another, I remain constant in the understanding of who I am.

It is always "I am" first, before any changing adjectives that follow. My awareness ensures that these roles or veils never alter or define me—they are simply the facades expected of me in the drama of life. I now take immense pleasure in my experiences, treating life as a theatre. I observe events, experiences, and circumstances without judgment, appreciating the richness they bring to the story.

Why Am I Writing This Book?

I humbly ask you to remain empty and non-judgmental since this book will challenge your beliefs, conditioning, and ego. I am writing this book so my children and grandchildren will walk my path to a better understanding of an effortless, tranquil, joyous, and peaceful life.

Unconditional happiness comes with a price, and the price is your mortal identity (the illusions involved, attached, judgmental, and biased individualistic personal identity). Once you self-realize and transcend the play of life and you are grounded in the unchanging, constant, permanent, and timeless True Self then you are liberated from the pains, fears, anxieties, and sufferings.

Just detach as an uninvolved, unbiased, nonjudgemental witness with all transient (everything impermanent) and remain aware of seeing everything come and go like you are watching the transient pixels on your screen come in and appear as a shape, color, and quality on the screen and just as easily disappear from the screen. The cost of losing your mortal individualistic personal identity comes with practice, resolute, earnestness, and hard work. The work can be easy, or for some, it can be harder than working out at the gym to get a fit body and six packs. Regardless, everyone wanting self-realization will do some work. If you want a fit body, you must go to the gym or do your workouts consistently no matter what. There is no way you can pay for the best trainer and achieve a fit body without some work involved. No trainer can do the work, and your body will achieve the benefit without you working on your body. So, I cannot help you by authoring this book or even holding your hand to self-realization without you wanting and walking the path and going within to contemplate.

My only hope is for you to find your own Truth. I am leaving you with these signposts for you to find your own path since I cannot walk your path for you. I know my only desire is to leave you a simple-to understand guidebook. Just like a recipe book, if you do not read, understand, follow, prepare, make a good effort, and cook the dish yourself, then it will not taste the same as the intended recipe.

I don't just want you to read and memorize the steps. I want you to dive in, understand, cook, and savor it for yourself. The journey to self-realization is like creating a masterpiece in the kitchen—you need to feel, experience, and truly live it. Know that in this form or beyond, I am always here, ready to support you as you find your own path to your own Truth. Seek self-realization with a burning desire and work towards achieving it, for the ultimate taste of life lies in discovering and embracing your true self.

Chapter 1

The Mirage of Identity

"Illusion is the first of all pleasures." Voltaire

Self is the image we have of ourselves. It is how we see ourselves through the interactions we have in this world with our families,

friends and other people who cross our paths. How we see ourselves is but an illusion, just a belief of who we are.

This "self" is shaped by belief systems, upbringing, cultural values, and societal norms. Across borders, religions, cultures, and educational systems, humans have built countless structures designed to condition children at an incredibly early age. These systems mold them into obedient followers, believers of ideas they often do not fully understand. As a result, from a young age, we become a "self" that we believe is our true self—but in reality, it is not.

Once programmed subconsciously, children grow into ideal materialistic consumers and compliant individuals who rarely question the accepted systems or truths—be they educational, financial, religious, societal, or cultural. They become followers, moving with the herd like sheep, blindly following where one leads. This phenomenon, identified by 19th-century social psychologists Gabriel Tarde and Gustave Le Bon as "herd mentality," is pervasive across the globe. I was no exception.

For much of my life, until my 40s, I never questioned these systems. I was an exemplary follower—obedient, respectful, and free of trouble at school, work, or in society. Yet, my life was governed by fear, rooted in the lessons instilled by my parents from an early age: "Cause and effect— every action has a consequence. Before you do anything, always be aware of its consequences." My father, too, lived his life conditioned by these teachings, never challenging the norms.

My father was an educated man who had seen the Western world. He graduated high school in the USA, earned a bachelor's degree from the

American University in Beirut, Lebanon, and held prominent positions at the United Nations in Kabul for over 15 years.

He was raised by my widowed grandmother, who lost her husband—my grandfather—when she was just 40. Despite never attending formal school, my grandmother was deeply knowledgeable, having learned from her father, a village mullah (priest). My grandfather, an orphan, became the primary caregiver for his three-year-old brother at just eight years old. He quit school to work and support them financially, ensuring his younger brother completed his education. His sacrifices paid off, as his brother earned a master's degree in psychology from Columbia University in the USA.

Both my father and his uncle were educated and worldly, proud Afghans who had experienced life beyond Afghanistan. In those days, only a fortunate few—either highly connected or exceptionally talented students—had the opportunity to travel to the West for education. My father was among this lucky group, and he cherished these opportunities.

Despite his education and exposure to the world, my father's subconscious mind remained deeply conditioned by his upbringing. As the saying goes, "You can take the boy out of the village, but you cannot take the village out of the boy." This was true for him. While he loved his country and was immensely proud of his heritage and culture, his early programming shaped his mindset in ways that even his advanced education and global experiences could not alter. His unwavering love for Afghanistan and its people ultimately drove his desire to return and contribute to building his homeland.

To his surprise, in 1977, the Soviet Union occupied Afghanistan, and anyone who had studied in the USA became a target. Despite the risks, my father, ever the patriot, refused to leave his homeland. Life under Soviet rule became a form of imprisonment. Every aspect of existence was consumed by propaganda, with the same lies repeated endlessly across all mediums. Over time, people began to accept these fabrications as facts and truths, turning brothers against brothers, sons against parents, friends against one another, and colleagues into enemies.

The Soviets employed the same divide, conquer, and control strategy used by the British in the past. When the military began unofficially drafting students as young as 14, panic set in. Everyone wanted to flee Afghanistan, though the chaos paled in comparison to the mass panic witnessed during the US exit from Afghanistan in 2021.

By my 40s, as the longing for self-investigation grew stronger, I began to see my past experiences as life lessons. These lessons, lived under Soviet occupation and through years of migration in search of a new home, shaped me profoundly. They granted me a unique ability: the capacity to embrace change with ease.

I believe this ability to adapt is one of the most vital skills in life. Everything in the universe is in constant flux—evolving and expanding. Resisting change goes against the very nature of the universe and our own humanity.

Ask yourself: Do you embrace change? Why is it so difficult to break old habits? Everyone has the right to change, to think critically, and to discover their own truths through personal experience. More importantly, everyone should be mindful of their subconscious mind and the habits it perpetuates.

I seek nothing from you except to guide you toward freedom from the mental suffering that binds you. I want the best for you and your children. I hope they never blindly accept any truth unless it becomes their own experiential reality. Read this book with an open heart, and if it doesn't resonate with you now, set it aside until it calls you back. Never force or resist anything. Surrender, and when the time is right, the transformation will come naturally.

This book aims to help you recognize and overcome the misidentification of the self with the selfless. It provides awareness, tools, and functions to guide you. First, you must realize that the self you know is an illusion—something you perceive but not your ultimate truth. It is simply a belief you've accepted as reality. To discover your true self, you must summon the courage to break through this illusion.

This book will equip you with the means to dismantle these false perceptions and embark on a journey to uncover your true self.

It does not matter how old or young you are. If this book speaks to you, do not walk away thinking it is not for someone your age. Age should not matter for self-investigation and self-inquiry. I became mindful of my subconscious mind and aware of my habits in my 40s. Staying empty helped me transcend more easily. Once I emptied myself, it became easier for me to transcend my conditioning, subconscious programming, and false identity.

My perception changed to unequivocal transparent knowingness (it started with belief, then turned into faith until it finally became experiential knowing) and liberation from old believed facts, bondage, and false truths. It was just like the elephant on the rope.

As a man was passing the elephants, he suddenly stopped, confused by the fact that these huge creatures were being held by only a small rope tied to their front leg. No chains, no cages. It was obvious that the elephants could, at any time, break away from their bonds, but for some reason, they did not. He saw a trainer nearby and asked why these animals just stood there and made no attempt to get away.

"Well," the trainer said, "when they are very young and much smaller, we use the same sized rope to tie them, and, at that age, it's enough to hold them. As they grow up, they are conditioned to believe they cannot break away. They believe the rope can still hold them, so they never try to break free.

The man was amazed. These animals could at any time break free from their bonds but because they believed they couldn't, they were stuck right where they were.[1]

We are not very different from these elephants. We keep believing that our self is the one we grew up with. It is permanent, it is who we are, and there's no changing it. I am here to tell you we couldn't be more wrong. How we are molded while growing up is not how we are supposed to stay for the rest of our existence in this world. We must search for our best and true self.

---

[1] Thanh Min, 2017. https://medium.com/motivationapp/the-elephant-rope-c22ee790a226

Chapter 2

Truth Beyond Illusion

"Truth is like the sun. You can shut it out for a time, but it ain't goin' away."~

Elvis Presley

Truth is often perceived as an immutable force, likened to the sun in Elvis Presley's metaphor. It's a concept that cannot be easily disregarded despite attempts to do so. But what is truth, really?

The essence of Truth has been a subject of contemplation and debate across centuries and civilizations. Often perceived as an absolute—a beacon of certainty in a world full of ambiguity—Truth reveals itself to be far more complex upon deeper exploration. It is not merely an objective reality waiting to be uncovered but a rich tapestry of individual experiences, cultural narratives, and evolving knowledge. This multifaceted nature of Truth invites us to question, explore, and embrace the diversity of perspectives that shape our understanding of reality.

Truth is not a fixed, universal constant; rather, it is a fluid, subjective construct. It evolves from the myriad influences that shape our perceptions and beliefs. From a young age, individuals are imprinted with various values and ideas, forming the foundation upon which their understanding of Truth is built. This foundation is as diverse as the cultures, religions, and societies that nurture it, leading to an array of personal truths that can differ vastly from one person to another.

The complexity of Truth lies in its inherent subjectivity. While some find their Truth in religious doctrines, others derive it from scientific inquiry or cultural heritage. Each person's Truth reflects their unique journey and the experiences that have shaped their worldview. This is why it is often said that everyone holds their own version of the Truth, shaped by the lens through which they perceive the world.

The subjective nature of Truth does not diminish its value. On the contrary, it highlights the importance of understanding and respecting the diverse perspectives each individual holds. By acknowledging that Truth is not singular but multifaceted, we can foster a more inclusive and empathetic society—one where differing beliefs and values are not merely tolerated but celebrated for the richness they bring to the human experience.

The search for Truth is a deeply personal and transformative journey. It requires the courage to question long-held beliefs, the curiosity to seek new knowledge, and the openness to embrace change. This journey is not about arriving at a single, unchanging Truth but about continually evolving and refining one's understanding of the world and oneself. In this sense, Truth is not a destination but a lifelong process of discovery and growth.

Part of the beauty of Truth lies in its multiplicity. Everyone's Truth is unique, shaped by a combination of beliefs, values, and facts absorbed from society, culture, science, and religion. The diversity of truths arises from the varied environments in which people are raised and the different experiences they encounter. These factors merge to create a distinctive perspective for each individual, further illustrating the fluidity and subjectivity of Truth.

This underscores the importance of continually re-evaluating and questioning the beliefs and values ingrained in us. Blindly accepting societal norms without scrutiny perpetuates falsehoods, undermining the integrity of both our personal and collective truths.

It is vital to approach life with an open mind, embracing new ideas, truths, and paradigms while avoiding attachment to any single belief. Attachment to ideas can hinder growth, trapping us in rigid perspectives and preventing us from uncovering deeper truths. By remaining open and adaptable, like water, we create space for intellectual and spiritual evolution.

Consider this: you came into this world with nothing. Whatever you fiercely protect as "yours" was never truly yours—it is an inherited idea from the environment in which you were raised. The beliefs and concepts we hold tightly often originate from family, culture, and society, rather than from our own experiences. Recognizing this allows us to detach from these inherited notions and embark on a journey to discover our own truths.

Personal truth must be realized through personal experience and introspection. Unless you have examined and embraced an idea as truly your own—after questioning its validity and understanding its significance—it remains an illusion. Living under the weight of inherited beliefs is living under illusions crafted by others, not the reality of your own making.

Later in this chapter, under the section Exhibit A, we will explore various examples of truths believed by millions for centuries, only to be later disproven. These examples highlight that repetition by the majority does not make an idea true; only your own experience can validate it as reality. This is why I urge you to keep an open mind and question your reality.

History is replete with instances of widely accepted truths that were eventually debunked. These serve as reminders of the necessity of personal inquiry and experiential knowledge in our search for deeper understanding and authenticity.

Unfortunately, though, most humans are trained to accept a comfortable lie rather than to seek an uncomfortable truth. By nature, humanity has accepted and adapted to feel comfortable in a commonly accepted safe lie rather than to change in the discomfort of unfamiliar truth. It is human nature to seek comfort and avoid discomfort, which often leads to the acceptance of falsehoods simply because they are easier to live with. **Exhibit A**

1. "Medieval scholars thought the Earth was flat. Like the geocentric model, the theory of a flat Earth dates back to antiquity, when many ancient cultures believed the Earth's shape resembled that of a flat disk. Many of these early beliefs had their root in creation myths – for example, one Homeric account from Ancient Greece said that the Earth was a disk floating on the ocean of Okeanos, a mystic being that created both the world and the gods. However, by the 5th century BCE, many philosophers had begun to gather empirical evidence that the world was instead a sphere, and the belief had largely died out in the Western world by the second century BCE. Despite these centuries of evidence, today, there are still many who subscribe to the "Flat Earth Society," claiming the world is, in fact, on a flat plane."

This example illustrates the remarkable persistence of deeply ingrained beliefs, even in the face of overwhelming evidence to the contrary. Despite living in an age of scientific enlightenment and technological advancement, there remains a subset of individuals who steadfastly adhere to the outdated notion of a flat Earth. Their unwavering commitment to this belief demonstrates the extraordinary power of entrenched convictions and the resistance to change inherent in human psychology.

Despite centuries of empirical evidence and scientific discoveries confirming the Earth's spherical nature, the flat Earth belief endures. This phenomenon underscores the profound influence of cultural, social, and psychological factors in shaping worldviews. It also highlights the considerable challenge of dispelling deeply rooted misconceptions, even when confronted with overwhelming scientific consensus.

The persistence of the flat Earth belief serves as a poignant reminder of the complexities of human cognition and the limitations of rationality in shaping belief systems. It prompts us to reflect on the influence of societal norms, personal biases, and cognitive dissonance in perpetuating beliefs that defy empirical evidence.

2. "One of the most well-known scientific myths, the geocentric model purported that the universe (including the Sun, stars, Moon, and other planets) revolved around the Earth. The model dates back to ancient societies and was supported by great philosophers like Aristotle and Ptolemy. The theory, bolstered by the casual observance that the Sun seemed to revolve around the Earth during the day, persisted despite the existence of the heliocentric theory (of planets revolving around the Sun). Its persistence was largely due to the support of religious sects. However, by the 16th century, many scientists began to accept and spread the heliocentric theory made popular by Copernicus."

The endurance of the geocentric model serves as a poignant reminder of the influence that authoritative figures and established institutions can wield over society's beliefs. Despite the emergence of compelling evidence supporting the heliocentric theory, the geocentric model persisted for centuries, bolstered by the support of prominent philosophers and religious sects. This enduring belief underscores the need for individuals to exercise critical thinking and skepticism, particularly in matters where authoritative voices may be inclined to preserve existing paradigms.

The case of the geocentric model exemplifies the complexities involved in challenging deeply ingrained beliefs. Even as scientific advancements provided mounting evidence against the geocentric view, its persistence reflects the resistance to change ingrained within societal structures. The reluctance to abandon established beliefs, especially those endorsed by influential institutions, highlights the formidable barriers that individuals face when confronted with contradictory evidence. Ultimately, the endurance of the geocentric model underscores the importance of fostering a culture of inquiry and critical examination of prevailing beliefs.

3.   "The Earth Orbits Around the Sun. Actually, the Earth does not orbit around the Sun. Cathy Jordan, a Cornell University Ask an Astronomer contributor, explains: "Technically, what is going on is that the Earth, Sun, and all the planets are orbiting around the center of mass of the solar system," she writes. "The center of mass of our solar system is very close to the Sun itself, but not exactly at the Sun's center."

The example of challenging established scientific truths serves as a compelling reminder of the dynamic nature of knowledge and understanding. While certain scientific principles may be widely accepted as incontrovertible, they are not immune to scrutiny or revision when confronted with new evidence or perspectives. This underscores the importance of maintaining healthy skepticism and a willingness to reevaluate our beliefs, even those that seem firmly established.

This example highlights the inherent complexity of scientific inquiry. Scientific truths are not static entities but evolving frameworks shaped by ongoing exploration and discovery. By embracing the provisional nature of scientific knowledge, we can cultivate a more nuanced understanding of the world and remain open to new insights that may challenge or refine existing paradigms.

The case of challenging established scientific truths illustrates the necessity of fostering a culture of intellectual humility and curiosity. These examples serve as potent reminders that our understanding of truth is not fixed but dynamic—subject to revision and refinement as our knowledge evolves. What we accept as truth today may be challenged and disproven tomorrow, reinforcing the importance of humility and open-mindedness in our pursuit of knowledge.

I hold the utmost respect for all religions and spiritual teachings, as I view them as attempts to articulate perceptions of the same Truth—one that transcends words and concepts. Anything verbalized, described, or conceptualized cannot capture Absolute Truth but represents a personal effort to provide signposts or directions toward realizing one's Truth.

Religious and spiritual teachings throughout history have offered wisdom and guidance to seekers on their journey toward Truth. Prophets and sages did not present their teachings merely for intellectual understanding or memorization. Instead, they aimed to inspire transparent knowing and direct human beings to experientially witness Truth. Their teachings pointed the way toward transcending tendencies, habits, memories (karmic, genetic, subconscious, and conscious), imaginations, the mind, and the body, encouraging individuals to become living evidence of the Truth itself.

My Truth is quite simple and transparent. Anyone with an open heart can be the evidence of it. At the beginning of my journey, I surrendered everything. Learned and remained as knowing, not physical nor mental, but intuitive, innate knowing, which is called the self-aware. It exists without any dependence on my body and mind. It is the observer within me. I just had to become a part of it.

Amidst this journey of self-discovery, I stumbled upon a profound tale known as "The Story of Truth & Lie."

One day, a man named Truth and a man named Lie stood by a river just outside of town. They were twin brothers. Lie challenged Truth to a race, claiming he could swim across the river faster than Truth. Lie laid out the rules to the challenge, stating that they both must remove all their clothes and, at the count of 3, dive into the freezing cold water and swim to the other side and back. Lie counted to 3, but when Truth jumped in, Lie did not. As Truth swam across the river, Lie put on Truth's clothes and walked back into town dressed as Truth. He proudly paraded around town pretending to be Truth. Truth made it back to shore, but his clothes were gone, and he was left naked with only Lie's clothes to wear. Refusing to dress himself as Lie, Truth walked back to town naked. People stared and glared as naked Truth walked through town. He tried to explain what happened and that he was, in fact, Truth, but because he was naked and uncomfortable to look at, people mocked and shunned him, refusing to believe he was really Truth. The people in town choose to believe Lie because he was dressed appropriately and easier to look at. From that day until this, people have come to believe a lie rather than believe a naked truth.[2]

This poignant allegory serves as a testament to the challenges we face in discerning truth from falsehood. In a world where appearances often deceive and illusions masquerade as reality, it is the naked truth that remains steadfast and unwavering. Just as Truth persevered despite the mockery and disbelief, so too must we remain committed to seeking truth, even when it is uncomfortable or inconvenient, for it is only through embracing the naked truth that we can truly find liberation and understanding in our journey of self-discovery.

---

[2] ZeroPark30,' The Story of Truth & Lie'.
https://medium.com/@ParkerSimpson/the-story-of-truth-lie1476bda2d45e

Chapter 3

Unmasking the True Self

"The ultimate truth is so simple; it is nothing more than being in one's natural, original state. "~

Ramana Maharshi

The concept of the True Self is often seen as a profound yet elusive notion. In our journey towards understanding the True Self, Ramana Maharshi's words invite us to contemplate beyond the transient identities we assume in daily life. The concept of the True Self transcends the limitations of the ego and mind, offering a glimpse into our eternal essence.

What exactly is this True Self? It exists before the notion of "I am," before the mind and its functions, before the body and its operations, even before the world and existence itself. The True Self is ultimate knowingness—devoid of judgment, contrast, experience, wants, or needs. It is formless, shapeless, birthless, deathless, effortless, peaceful, and joyous. The True Self mirrors the ultimate singularity that halts the "I am" in deep sleep. It resembles the ultimate black hole, drawing everything towards it, allowing nothing to escape.

We often forget the infinite self within, becoming engrossed in pleasing the limited, imagined, impermanent self we identify with. Immersed in this divine play, we completely misidentify our True Self. The divine design is so intricate that it keeps everyone occupied; even a genius can't realize they are merely playing a role in the theater of life. This realization depends not on IQ but on EQ—it is realized by the heart, not the mind, which is why billions miss it, though it is so clear to sages, prophets, and seers.

It's best to cease the struggle and surrender completely to the True Self, accepting the ultimate Absolute Truth as our inevitable destiny.

The thirst and yearning guided me to discover my path to One Awareness, and I wish the same for you. I was drawn to realize my True Self in this life, while in the warmth of my body and mind. I feared suffering and the unknown after death for eternity, so it was an obvious choice to realize the Self while alive in the warmth of the body.

It was an obvious choice to realize the Self while alive in the warmth of the body so I could truly be life rather than merely have a life. Also, to transition to death with dignity, peacefully and effortlessly.

I surrendered and abided as the True Self, allowing all my conditioning, ego, personality, mind, and functions to fade away. They visit occasionally, but now they remain weak as obedient servants, understanding that every kingdom can have only one king.

Last week, while driving home, someone cut me off and flipped me off without any apparent reason. My ego urged me to react, but I remained a witness to my ego, and it quietly dissipated on the horizon. Such instances are common in our daily lives. How we respond to them defines us.

Do you want to hear something astounding? I had always believed and misidentified my false identity, false truths, and false conditioning, resisting the obvious. The Truth becomes evident when people from different religions, cultures, and historical periods share the same experiential truths.

The obvious truth is akin to science: anyone who undertakes self-investigation transparently and clearly realizes it, regardless of race, culture, nationality, religion, or circumstance. Yet, most people, especially scientists, may not accept it, as it lies beyond their experience and capacity.

"A scientific fact results from repeated careful observation or measurement through experimentation or other means, known as empirical evidence. These are fundamental to building scientific theories."

This is the definition of a scientific fact, and I can affirm that without the requisite qualifications to conduct a scientific experiment, no one can achieve identical results as empirical evidence, no matter how many times they attempt the same experiment under identical conditions. Clearly, scientists and unqualified individuals who engage in meditation cannot immediately experience transcendence. It requires time, maturity, and practice to transcend empirically from body and mind.

Give me ten scientists who are willing to empty themselves of concepts, memories, and imagination and who will engage in self-inquiry for the same duration it takes to earn a Ph.D. Then, I will allow them to judge the realization of the True Self.

I gained clarity when I saw through the veil of time, realizing how sages, seers, and prophets from diverse parts of the world, across different eras, some unaware of each other's existence or concepts, described the same Ultimate Absolute Self Essence:

Rumi's Farsi text: "I have lived on the lip of insanity, wanting to know reasons, knocking on a door. It opens. I've been knocking from the inside."

"I am the Truth. (Ana Al-Haqq (Arabic: أنا الحقيقة*)).* " **- Mansur Al-Hallaj quote.**

"What we are looking for is what is looking."

- St. Francis of Assisi

"I don't have a life, but I am the same life essence in existence, present in every being."

-RZ

"One day you will ask me which is more important? My life or yours? I will say mine and you will walk away not knowing that you are my life."

-Khalil Gibran quote.

"There is no "I" as such apart from others. The reality of nature, the reality of life is oneness. But we humans have such a strong egotistic nature." **-Buddha.**

Understanding this profound teaching requires us to delve deeper into how we can identify our True Self.

Finding Your True Self

Identifying the True Self involves peeling away layers of conditioning and false identification that obscure our innate essence. Here are some fundamental aspects to consider:

- Begin by questioning who or what you truly are beyond your name, roles, body, mind, and identities. Ramana Maharshi's method of self-inquiry—asking "Who am I?"—can lead you beyond superficial layers of identity to a deeper understanding. Transcend the layers of veils and masks and prioritize the permanent, constant, and aware origin of transients.

- The True Self is not the mind nor the derivatives of the mind but the observer behind them. Practice observing your thoughts without judgment or attachment. Recognize that you are the awareness that witnesses' thoughts come and go.

- The ego is the false self that thrives on separation and identification with roles and achievements. Letting go of ego involves relinquishing attachment to these identities and realizing that they are transient and not the core of who you are.

- Recognize that your True Self is interconnected with all existence. Just as the ocean is made up of countless drops, our individual selves are expressions of the same universal consciousness or Oneness.

- The True Self transcends dualities such as good/bad, right/wrong, and success/failure. It exists in a state of pure being beyond conceptual distinctions.

- Cultivate moments of inner stillness and silence where the True Self can be felt rather than conceptualized. In these moments, there is a sense of peace, expansiveness, and unity with everything.

- While the mind analyzes and categorizes, the True Self is felt intuitively through the heart. Develop heart-centered awareness through practices like compassion, gratitude, and unconditional love.

- Accepting the present moment fully and surrendering to what is allows the True Self to emerge naturally. Resistance to what creates inner conflict and perpetuates the illusion of separateness.

- The realization of the True Self is not just a philosophical concept but a lived experience. Integrate this understanding into everyday actions, relationships, and challenges.

Living from the awareness of the True Self means embodying this realization in every aspect of life. It's about aligning thoughts, words, and actions with the recognition that the essence of who we are transcends the temporary identities and roles we play. By doing so, we cultivate harmony, compassion, and authenticity in our interactions and decisions, paving the way for a life rooted in inner peace and wisdom.

According to the famous psychoanalyst Sigmund Freud, the id is the primitive and instinctual part of the mind that contains aggressive drives and hidden memories, the superego operates as a moral conscience, and the ego is the realistic part that mediates between the desires of the id and the superego.

Although this theory has been debunked since its introduction, people still use these terminologies to define the distinct parts of themselves – the one that desires, the one that manages those desires, and the one that shuns all desire. I refer to these identities within our identity as nothing but mental constructs of our minds. We can make or break these "identities."

Because we are not our minds; the mind is a minuscule imagined part of the Self. The mind itself does not exist; it is a psychological function of the brain and can only exist when the brain is in action. The mind exists only when the brain is awake or during the dream state of the cognitive psychological brain. During deep sleep, when the cognitive psychological brain is dormant, the mind disappears with memory, thoughts, identity, and imagination.

I am the True Self without contrast, detached from all earthly things, in singularity, transcending the existence, space, and time realm in deep sleep. In deep sleep, awareness remains as no(thing), self-aware, and at ultimate peace, tranquility, and joy.

That is why, during the wakened state and dream state, we suffer from our experiences. Humans have false identities; we falsely identify with and as impermanent. Everything but the Truth is impermanent and transient, including space, time, and universes. The transient impermanent can only exist through contrast and duality. We need to transcend our false identities and permanently identify as the permanent True Self.

I am the black hole with invincible powers attracting and transforming everything, including you and me (personal identities), into nothing or singularity. It is a matter of time whether you (egoistic identity) like it or not; your final destiny is in singularity. It is best to realize the singularity within you while in this body, mind, space, and time. I am the black hole singularity or nothingness that swallows everything from the birth of time to the end of time. Tomorrow, when the impermanent (everything including my body, mind, space, and time) evanesce, I remain unchanged, permanent, and absolute in singularity. I am nothing, and I am everything.

Like the black hole in singularity, the physical, quantum physical, and metaphysical, from the biggest to the smallest, becomes absolute in singularity.

The root of all problems with humanity is our identification with our selfish, egoistic, and individualistic false personal identity. We are programmed to identify with a false personal identity which is a result of our conditioning since childhood.

Humans love to dissect everything to find the roots and composition of everything, and yet, when it comes to our true existence, we neglect to dissect ourselves to find what we are a product of.

Please look inside to inquire and reflect on finding the answer to this question, what are we products of?

We love to identify effortlessly with our personality, ego, egoistic identity, body, and mind because that is easier than digging deep into our consciousness. Let us not be afraid of what lies on the other side; let's dig deep to find out what produced this body and mind.

The body, mind, and their reactions are mere functions that we identify as, and they are products of our minds; they are not who we are. Look deeper and it becomes obvious that our brain is a part of our physical body. This physical body is a product of food that we consume, which is a byproduct of the Earth (water, dirt, air, fire, and space).

Consume a piece of bread, an apple, meat, or veggies, and in a few hours, it becomes your body. Food is not considered by our body until consumed and digested. The food that we eat is a product of this Earth; we are what we eat, so we are the Earth and everything that exists on this planet. We are the children of Mother Earth.

Without Mother Earth, we cannot exist, animals, plants, trees, and no life can exist. So, don't be so egoistic and individualistic to believe that humans are not one with and dependent on the Earth, the same way if I falsely believed that I could live without my respiratory or digestive system.

Most sea creatures cannot live without seawater, so half of their gills or respiratory system is the sea. All mammals rely on oxygen in the air, or we all die. It is obvious that half our lungs are trees and vegetation. Half of my digestive system is the food provided by this Earth. Most importantly, 100% of my body is made from and made on the Earth. I rely much more on Mother Earth than she relies on my body, but I am not my body. I just borrowed my body from Mother Earth for a short time to experience heaven on Earth as the spirit.

Every ounce of this body borrowed from Earth must return to Earth; anything gained (the body, mind, and ego) and learned from this dimension belongs here and cannot be taken. It is a waste; we take so much pride in our bodies, minds, and egos when, in fact, we all know the impermanent is not ours to take. Don't take pride in your humanity or its representations. Only stay humble in your unrealized, true, formless, timeless self, your spirit, which is closer than your breath and heartbeat to you.

Now let us zoom out further, Mother Earth is a product of our solar system. The solar system is a product of the cosmos, and the cosmos came from no(thing) or nothingness (The Big Bang). The Big Bang was born from the shapeless, formless, limitless, infinite, timeless, and spaceless fundamental field of energy that manifested everything.

Upon reflection within, we realize that everything is One, where everything is just the derivative of The One, we came from the One which is expanding as One in the Oneness.

On the quantum level, everything is limitless, made of the exact same protons, neutrons, electrons, up quarks, down quarks, photons, strange quarks, muons, positrons, and alpha particles. On a macro level, everything, including you and me, is made of and is pure awareness.

It is a pity that we are still identifying ourselves as our individual selfish and egocentric minds and bodies, identifying as our mere psychologically created false identities. The cognitive mind, our psyche, and individual identities are a mere minuscule reflection of our True Self.

I realized that the person I thought I was all my life never existed. It only existed in my mind and, memory, and imagination. Take out my imagination and memory then where can I find this person who I thought I was? The mind is nothing but a collection of thoughts, emotions, memory, imagination, sensations, and a plain cognitive psychological brain in action.

The brain has more reality than the person in my mind because the brain is at least physical, and the person in my mind is not even physical but just the brain in action. Anything derived from my mind is just a derivative of it and, therefore, cannot exist. It exists as a function of my self-awareness, and there is nothing wrong with it if I do not identify myself as the function itself.

My feelings, emotions, thoughts, imagination, perceptions of sensations, fears, worries, wants, needs, desires, temptations, discomforts, impatience, ego, identity, and personality are all derivatives of my mind. Since the mind is just a brain in action, an illusion, then all its derivatives are just not real; they are an illusion, and they are evolutionary functions of my mind subconsciously programmed in my genetic memory.

Our genes are programmed to reward and punish the cognitive psychological identity to promote and attract to identify as the mind and its derivatives. The mind and mind derivatives' objective are to promote our body and mind's longevity, the chance of survival, and advantageous spawning.

There is nothing wrong with the mind or its functions if we just do not misidentify it. My body is designed to use my mind and its functions to advance my chances on Earth. My body, mind, and its functions are my evolutionary progression through the process of elimination. It has an award and punishment system through which programs my genes as far as what to pass on to the next generation.

In the same way, an actor wants to have better tools for acting to play his role in a movie. I doubt if any actor would take his/her role so seriously to identify as his role or his acting tools.

I use my body and mind as tools, but I no longer identify myself as them. Every morning, before getting out of bed, I accept and appreciate my body and its functions—breathing, walking, seeing, tasting, hearing, and more. With gratitude for these blessings, I set my intention for the day as a blessed one for me and my family.

Gratitude has become a transformative practice in my life. In the presence of gratitude, negativity cannot take root. I cannot feel anger, emptiness, frustration, inadequacy, helplessness, fear, guilt, loneliness, sadness, jealousy, hatred, or resentment when I am truly grateful.

Do you remember how, every morning while driving you to school, I preached to you about the power of gratitude? I wasn't just speaking to fill the silence—I want you to feel and practice gratitude every day. Make it a part of your life.

I lost so much of my life when I falsely identified with my feelings, emotions, thoughts, fears, and anxieties. I drove myself to the brink, believing I would die if I didn't take my anxiety pills. Days before I ran out of medication, I would already be consumed by fear. I became a slave to my pills, anxieties, and fears.

But these fears were nothing more than thoughts in my head. At best, they were my imagination running wild. My thoughts fed my emotions, and my emotions fueled my thoughts, creating a vicious cycle that spiraled out of control. Over time, my body began to expect this constant drama, becoming addicted to the chemicals produced by my worries, fears, and anxieties—what Eckhart Tolle calls the "pain-body." It was a helpless cycle.

I broke free by refusing to feed those negative thoughts. Instead, I used tools to keep myself anchored in the present moment—biking, walking, swimming, and taking hot showers, playing chess, cards, and writing. These activities became lifelines, grounding me in the now and helping me disrupt the cycle of fear and anxiety.

It feels foolish to admit all of this to you, but I am not ashamed. Sharing my past may help you if you ever find yourself in a similar place of hopelessness. My hope is that you learn from my struggles and discover your own tools and practices to remain present, grateful, and at peace.

Breaking Free from Mental Illusions

The mind is highly creative and will conjure countless versions of the True Self. The ego, in particular, can manipulate this process. It may inflate itself, playing the role of the True Self, and convince you that you are an extraordinary super-being, capable of anything from a personal perspective. If unchecked by awareness, this can lead to a dangerous path of narcissism. Alternatively, the ego may take the opposite approach, making you feel guilty and unworthy of receiving the True Self. It will fight relentlessly to keep you from realizing your actual True Self, using every tool at its disposal.

My ego played these games with me on every level—emotionally, mentally, physically, and psychologically. In the solitude of my room, I'd find myself laughing uncontrollably one moment and crying the next, with no discernible reason. Out in public, it was even more challenging. I remember sitting with you both at lunch, and out of nowhere, I would burst into tears and run to the bathroom. You were so young at the time, staring at me with bewildered expressions, not understanding what had just happened. Truthfully, neither did I.

It felt like a wave of dark, uncontrollable emotions washing over me—a desperate act of resistance from the ego-mind. The ego sensed its inevitable demise the moment I discovered my True Self and began to unite with Oneness.

Realizing the True Self is not difficult; in fact, it's effortless. The challenge lies in navigating the ego's illusions. The ego-mind creates the false perception that discovering the True Self is an impossible, elusive journey. But once you see through this illusion, the path becomes clear.

Remaining stuck in the seeker's ego-self means never truly attaining, seeing, or understanding Awareness. If you cling to being a seeker, prepare for a long journey. It's crucial to transcend both the seeker and the act of seeking, as they are fundamentally the same. True existence flourishes because the True Self is aware of my body, mind, bodily functions, and mental processes. My reality's existence ebbs and flows within this awareness. When you become ensnared by the ego mind and fixate on it, the True Self remains elusive, hidden behind the shadows and distractions of the ego. As I reflect on my journey towards realizing the True Self, there is a timeless tale that resonates deeply with this quest. It's a story passed down through generations, known as "The Tale of the Wise Gardener."

Once upon a time, in a small village nestled between rolling hills and lush forests, there lived a wise gardener named Kai. Kai was renowned for his ability to grow the most vibrant and beautiful flowers in his garden. People from neighboring villages would come to marvel at the colors and fragrances that seemed to dance in harmony under Kai's care. One day, a traveler passing through the village heard about Kai's garden and decided to pay him a visit. As the traveler walked along the cobblestone path that led to Kai's home, he couldn't help but notice the tranquil atmosphere that surrounded the garden. Birds sang joyfully, and a gentle breeze carried the sweet scent of flowers. Upon reaching Kai's home, the traveler found him tending to a small patch of roses. The roses, vibrant in hues of red, pink, and white, swayed gracefully in the breeze. Intrigued by Kai's serene demeanor, the traveler struck up a conversation. "Your garden is truly magnificent," the traveler remarked, "but what is your secret, Kai? How do you grow such beautiful flowers?" Kai smiled warmly and gestured for the traveler to sit beside him on a weathered wooden bench overlooking the garden. "It's not about what I do, but how I see," Kai explained. "Long ago, I realized that each flower has its own essence, its own unique beauty. I stopped trying to make them grow in a certain way or look a certain way. Instead, I simply provide them with what they need—nourishment, sunlight, and care." The traveler listened intently, captivated by Kai's words. "Each flower," Kai continued, "is like a mirror reflecting back the beauty of the garden. Just as the garden thrives when each flower blooms in its own way, so too does our true nature shine when we let go of expectations and simply allow ourselves to be." The traveler pondered Kai's words as they strolled through the garden together. As they reached the end of the garden path, Kai stopped beside a small pond where a single lotus flower floated gracefully on the water's surface. "This lotus," Kai said softly, "teaches me every day about the nature of our true selves. It grows from the mud at the bottom of the pond, yet its petals remain unstained by the mud. In the same way, our true selves are untouched by the challenges and distractions of the world around us." The traveler nodded in understanding, feeling a sense of peace wash over him. He realized that, like Kai's flowers and the lotus in the pond, each person carries within them a seed of pure potential—their True Self—waiting to bloom in its own time and way.

This profound tale of the Wise Gardener serves as a poignant reminder of the challenges encountered in the quest for selfrealization. In a world where illusions often obscure reality and perceptions can be misleading, it is the essence of truth that endures unwavering and resolute. Just as the True Self was unveiled amidst the gardener's patient nurturing, so too must we cultivate patience and awareness on our own paths of self-discovery. Through letting go of illusions and embracing our innate essence, we uncover a deep-seated tranquility and wisdom within. This journey calls not for acquiring something new but for unveiling the eternal presence that lies dormant within each of us—a presence that transcends the ephemeral identities and fluctuations of the mind.

Chapter 4

The Journey Within

"Go within, and you will never go without." ~

Yogi Bhajan

Our universe and everything in it, including us, are manifestations of awareness within a unified Oneness. This fundamental field of awareness is everyone's unrealized hidden Beingness. I want to share how I came to this realization. For the longest time, I couldn't understand this until one day, I emptied my mind and focused all my senses to only listen to my heartbeat. With practice, I did hear my heartbeat, which was always there—I can't even live without it.

Before this, I couldn't hear my heartbeat because my mind was too busy with external things, the thoughts in my mind, and the happenings around me. The heartbeat sends 20,000 gallons of blood to every cell of my body daily to help me oxygenate every cell of my body. Every cell of my body counts on every beat of my heart, yet I was so unaware of it all because I was too attached and identified with external things and thoughts. It's like being inside a nightclub with too many things happening around you in a crowd with extremely loud music, making it impossible to hear anyone or anything but loud music. The minute you want to talk to an interesting person, you block all the distractions, and if you focus enough on that person, you can hear them.

In contemplation, I go within to slow down my mind and put the attention of my focus on being and feeling rather than doing and thinking, so I'm able to remain as my True Self without the projections and delusions of my mind. I don't have any proof or magic to show you, but I know it from my own experience of going within and reflecting. I am no different from any of you, so if I can go within and remain my True Self, then you can do the same. No one can just mentally understand this state without going within themselves, meditating, and contemplating mindfully to transcend the transient and remain as True Self in Oneness.

To go within means to drop everything (concepts, memory, imagination, thoughts) and remain empty but Aware. The True Self is within, all around, and everywhere. It's a field of timeless and shapeless invisible energy that holds all energy, all matter, and dark matter in our Universe, time & space, multiverses, and multidimensions in existence. Like the invisible magnetic field that holds this universe together and in existence. With the advancement of technology and science, we will be able to prove that Awareness is the fundamental field of manifestation in existence.

This same field of Grace existed before the Big Bang, manifesting our universe—a field of knowingness, awareness, and grace that brings everything into existence. The greater Self, the pure awareness, "Grace," is all One, and everything we perceive is a projection of it. Let me share a concept drawn from my own experience.

Imagine your consciousness as an expansive field, dotted with countless kites soaring high above, each one tethered by a thread. These threads are more than mere attachments—they represent the focus of your attention, tied to various aspects of your mental landscape: thoughts, feelings, fears, worries, anxieties, emotions, memories, perceptions, imaginations, experiences, and sensations.

The kites that occupy more of your attention have stronger threads, intensifying your experience of them. Yet, you hold the power to sever these threads, letting the kites drift away, or to strengthen them into ropes by focusing even more attention on them. This dynamic interplay—all of it—exists within the bubble of your witnessing Awareness.

Your consciousness is a unified field that encompasses physical, quantum, and metaphysical realities. While it depends on the physical body, mind, and spirit for expression, it transcends them through its Awareness.

Picture consciousness as a radiant full moon. Its beauty and presence are undeniable, but it relies on the light of the sun to shine. Similarly, your consciousness is a powerful co-creator, shaping your ego, emotions, thoughts, perceptions, identity, and personality. It acts as a bridge, connecting you to the external world while guiding you inward toward the realization of your spiritual self within the localized bubble of awareness.

This field of Grace, the foundation of everything, is always present. It is both the source and the guide, showing you the way to transcend the threads of attachment and recognize your true nature as One with the expansive field of Awareness.

According to Neville Goddard, imagination and consciousness are the building blocks of our reality. He emphasized the power of imagining and feeling as though your desires are already fulfilled, shaping your experience of the world. In this context, the kites represent the myriad thoughts and emotions vying for your attention. By focusing on certain kites—those tied to your aspirations and positive imaginings—you can transform your reality. This is the essence of conscious manifestation.

The bubble of awareness is tethered to your existence within this time and space. When the physical body ceases to exist, the "you" tied to it dissolves, along with all the accumulated experiences. The localized bubble of awareness bursts, allowing consciousness to expand or reconnect with Pure Absolute Awareness. This cycle is universal, touching all beings, from the smallest insect to the most complex human. Just like a house is dismantled, revealing the space that existed before and remains after its demolition, so too does consciousness persist beyond the physical form.

The localized witness awareness is patient, non-judgmental, and unbiased. The localized witness awareness is like a computer game designer who remains passive, witnessing (a witness can't get involved, or he is not a legitimate witness) an AI self-developing game and letting the AI game create and advance its redevelopment to evolve until the game's over. Since the creator of the game knows it's just a game, there is no need to make it too difficult with too many rules; let it co-create its own rules as the game self-improves. The designer gives the game the power to let the individual avatars autonomously think and rewrite its code to learn, relearn, unlearn, program, and reprogram to improve itself with two fundamental criteria to improve and evolve: its chance of survival and strengthening its DNA by passing important evolutionary genes through reproduction. Each time the AI game self-improves, the game lasts longer. If the AI avatars become good co-creators as they were designed to be in the rescripted game, then the quality of life and expectancy increase.

It's a simple AI game with simple rules (survival of the fittest) and simple fundamentals to increase the chances of survival and improve life expectancy by passing the knowledge/memory (DNA) on to new avatars. The designer's fundamental goal is to give each player a chance to improve life qualities through the process of reward and punishment until the AI avatar realizes the Truth that it is just a preordained act in the game of the game maker's One Awareness.

You can see this example in action when you play a video game. Even the vague characters that don't seem to be doing much are planned to add more depth to the game and to give you suspicions about what your next steps should be. This is the aim of a good developer, to create such a design that carries itself without further coding required. AI works on principles of machine learning, more specifically, reinforcement learning. Reinforcement learning implies an agent learns how to behave in an environment by performing actions and getting feedback. It is like the way humans or even dogs learn in their early years: ***An action is taken → feedback is received (positive or negative) → conclusion*** is drawn based on the feedback, whether the action was good or bad. AI programs use similar structures. They learn much like us based on the experience/feedback they receive.

Another example is the field of radio frequencies. These frequencies are nearly everywhere on the surface of the Earth, yet without the right instruments—like a radio—you would never hear or even realize their presence. Even with the proper equipment, you won't always immediately get what you desire. Having a radio to tune into these frequencies doesn't guarantee you'll hear your favorite songs all the time; you'll need to adjust and wait until you align with the right frequencies.

It's okay if you don't grasp this concept right away. If something feels unclear, it's best to admit it and say, "I don't know enough about this subject, but I'm willing to learn." There is nothing wrong with acknowledging that you haven't yet had the experience to fully understand it. This acceptance is a crucial first step toward growth and learning.

Someone who refuses to acknowledge their need for knowledge closes themselves off to discovery. On the other hand, admitting you have more to learn opens the door to new understanding, deeper insights, and personal transformation.

There are many dimensions and multiverses beyond our own. Until we find the instruments to bring these dimensions into our experience, we can't simply reject them. Keep in mind these factors:

- All living beings are instruments of awareness, but humans are unique in their ability to self-realize this, Truth.

- Human beings can self-realize the field of awareness within, around, and everywhere. The source of all existence in the form of all existence.

- By inquiring, going within, staying empty of mind, and becoming one with the field of awareness, you can expand into this timeless and shapeless field.

- With years of practice, earnestness, and humility, you stop identifying with your mind, ego, and body, developing an expanded universal sensory system.

- The personal sensory system is limited, but the universal sensory system has no boundaries and is infinite.

- This universal sensory is your expanded awareness without boundaries, including everyone and everything as your true self.

- As True Awareness, you transcend attachments to personal interests, defensiveness, fears, worries, anxieties, and other limitations.

- The body and mind remain as tools for as long as you are alive, but they no longer define or hold you. You use them for the benefit of your body, mind, and circumstances.

With unconditional love and by letting go of mind-driven concepts, you can perceive the true essence of Awareness in everyone and everything. The desire for autonomous personal choice fades away, along with personal dreams, fears, anxieties, worries, perceptions, and imaginations. In this state, personal choice, karma, and the sense of individual doership dissolve, and actions arise naturally, not from personal will but from harmony with the universal flow. Even the body exists in awareness and equilibrium, in unity with everything and everyone.

When you embrace your expanded universal identity, you begin to see everyone and everything as an extension of yourself. The very thought of harming others or the Earth becomes inconceivable because the ego-driven sense of separateness no longer dominates. Intentions lose their personal significance because, in the realization of unity, acting for the collective good becomes as natural as protecting both your left and right eyes—they are one and the same.

Competition for personal gain becomes meaningless. Let animals engage in the game of survival and competition; humanity is destined for something greater. Once awakened to the Truth, humans are ready to play the transcendent game, a game rooted in unity, cooperation, and collective well-being. This shift marks a transition from the shadows of egoic veils and identities into the light of our true being.

Embracing life without attachments, judgments, insecurities, or fears leads to a profound transformation, allowing you to experience the joy of existence fully. Transitioning from a competitive to a transcendent way of living is a personal journey, and there is no need to rush—each individual progresses at their own pace. Ultimately, cooperation, not competition, will guide humanity toward a sustainable and harmonious future for our planet and all its inhabitants.

America holds immense potential to lead by example in this transformative journey. It begins with courageous individuals transcending their identities and embracing their true selves. Collective change starts within each person. Efforts to address issues like drug abuse, racism, equality, and justice must stem from personal transformation to resonate outward effectively and sustainably.

Imagine a world where Corporate America prioritizes equity for employees and customers over self-interest and shareholder returns. Fair and ethical practices would flourish as consumers naturally support companies that uphold equitable standards and work toward a fairer, more compassionate world.

This vision is not extraordinary but rooted in the practical wisdom of a transcendent universal self. It requires a gradual process, not an instant change, demanding conviction and determination to transcend personal identities and enact meaningful societal shifts over time. As you will see in the example below, it took years of experimentation until they found the Higgs Boson field at CERN.

To truly embrace this state, we must recognize that transcendence is not easy by any means. It requires determination, earnestness, and focus. The personal egoistic individual identity often feels entitled to everything and wants awakening to be served magically on a silver platter. The realization of the true self is effortless, but being too attached to your ego makes it difficult.

The fundamental field of Awareness eludes detection and measurement by any human-developed instrument. We must not dismiss this field simply because we lack the tools to bring it into our direct experience. A comparable example is the Higgs Boson field, which was hypothesized in 1964 by Peter Higgs, François Englert, and others to explain the origin of particle mass.

Stars, planets, and life emerged only when particles acquired mass from the Higgs boson field, confirmed by the discovery of the Higgs boson particle at CERN in 2012 [3]. This elusive particle, the last of the 17 elementary particles in the Standard Model of particle physics, took half a century to find and plays a crucial role in subatomic physics, often dubbed the "God particle." [4]

For a long time, the Higgs Boson field remained theoretical due to our lack of equipment. Simply put, the Higgs field gives mass to particles that would otherwise be massless, acting as a universal medium that differentiates particle masses.

Similarly, we recognize that invisible dark matter and dark energy constitute 95% of the universe, affecting light and gravity without direct observation. Named for their elusive nature, these entities are essential for explaining galaxy motions and universal structures despite being undetectable with current instruments.

Dark matter, first theorized by Fritz Zwicky in 1933 and supported by Vera Rubin's 1970s research, interacts only through gravity with visible matter, highlighting a substantial gap in our understanding of the universe's composition.

Thus, just as the Higgs field opened doors to exploring mass, dark matter and dark energy challenges us to expand our understanding of the universe beyond what our senses perceive.

To understand how deeply interconnected we are with the universe, consider the Big Bang Theory, the leading explanation for how the universe began. Simply put, it says the universe as we know started with an infinitely hot and dense single point that inflated and stretched.

---

[3] https://home.cern/science/physics/higgs-boson
[4] https://www.livescience.com/higgs-boson-particle

Hubble's discovery of farther galaxies moving away from us proved that the universe is indeed constantly expanding.

There are theories like string theory and loop quantum gravity. In these attempts, ordinary space and time are typically seen as emergent, like the waves on the surface of a deep ocean. What we experience as space and time are the products of quantum processes operating at a deeper, microscopic level—processes that don't make much sense to us as creatures rooted in the macroscopic world.

The field of awareness is timeless and boundless. Our universe, time, and space were manifested from this fundamental field as One and are expanding within this Oneness. No atom in the universe is not a part of the fundamental, timeless field of awareness. Everything, including the universe, all matter, dark matter, dark energy, you, and me, are small components of Awareness.

Quantum entanglement further illustrates our interconnectedness. "Entanglement is at the heart of quantum physics and future quantum technologies. Like other aspects of quantum science, the phenomenon of entanglement reveals itself at very tiny subatomic scales. When two particles, such as a pair of photons or electrons, become entangled, they remain connected even when separated by vast distances. In the same way that a ballet or tango emerges from individual dancers, entanglement arises from the connection between particles. It is what scientists call an emergent property." [5]

According to quantum entanglement, at the very early phase of the Big Bang, before any particle was created, the potential of every particle in the universe was One. The universe was born, inflated, and expanded from this Oneness, and all particles emerged from this unified state. Therefore, every particle in the universe is entangled and is One.

Perhaps the best way to understand this is through the parable of "The King and the Drop of Water." Just as the king learns from the monk that a single drop is inseparable from the vast stream, our individual experiences are transient forms within the boundless sea of consciousness.

---

[5] https://scienceexchange.caltech.edu/topics/quantum-science-explained/entanglement

"A king, burdened by the weight of his crown and the constant demands of his kingdom, felt a deep yearning for peace. He sought guidance from a wise old monk who lived on a mountaintop. The monk listened patiently as the king poured out his worries. Then, he led the king to a crystal-clear mountain stream. As a single drop of water trickled down a smooth rock, the monk asked, "Your Majesty, can you tell the difference between that drop of water and the vast stream above?" The king peered closely. "No, wise one," he admitted, "they appear to be the same." The monk smiled. "Indeed. Now, cup your hand and catch the drop." The king cupped his hand, and a single drop of water landed in his palm. He examined it, a tiny sphere glistening in the sunlight. "This drop," the monk continued, "is like your current experience. You are focused on the immediate concerns that weigh upon you. But remember, that drop is still part of the vast stream above. Just as the drop cannot exist without the stream, you cannot exist without the underlying field of pure awareness, the source of all existence." The king pondered this. He dipped his cupped hand back into the stream, allowing the drop to rejoin the flow. "Just as I release the drop back to the stream," the monk said, "you can release your worries and reconnect with the source of your being. Through meditation and inner reflection, you can learn to see beyond the transient experiences and connect with the infinite wellspring of peace and awareness that lies within you." The king returned to his palace with a newfound perspective. He began to practice meditation, quieting his mind and focusing on the stillness within. Slowly, he began to feel a sense of peace and connection that transcended his worldly concerns. He realized that his true self was not defined by his role as king but by his connection to the vast ocean of awareness from which all things arose."

Similarly, everything in the universe, including you, is like a drop in the crystal-clear stream of Pure Awareness. We perceive ourselves as separate entities with distinct experiences, but fundamentally, we are united with One Awareness. This realization is the essence of going within and connecting to Oneness.

In this Oneness, the illusion of separation dissolves. Just as the drop is never truly separate from the stream, we are never truly separate from the Awareness. This understanding brings about a profound sense of peace and unity. You recognize that your true essence transcends your physical body and personal identity, merging with the infinite and timeless Awareness that permeates everything.

The journey within involves shedding the layers of ego, identity, and mind-created boundaries to reconnect with this fundamental Awareness. It's about transcending the transient and embracing the eternal. When you authentically connect with this Oneness, you experience harmony, love, and a profound connection with all of existence. This is the ultimate realization of our true nature and the essence of the journey within.

Chapter 5

Purpose Beyond the Self

"The cosmos is within us. We are made of star stuff. We are a way for the universe to know itself." ~

Carl Sagan.

Everything and everyone in the universe have a role, and it's a beautiful symphony if we keep our ego and personal identity in check. Human beings' egos and individual identities are often the root of many human problems. Awareness, existence, and our universe were, are, and will be just fine without humanity or the world. Unfortunately, we humans tend to give ourselves immense undeserving credit for everything positive happening on Earth.

Our solar system is a speck of cosmic dust in the grandeur of the universe, and Earth itself is merely a speck of dust within our solar system. To put it into perspective, Earth makes up about 0.0003% of the total mass of our solar system. From the vastness of time and space, each human being is akin to a microscopic speck. Yet, with an inflated ego, this speck can press a button and potentially alter the lives of millions or even jeopardize our entire planet.

When comparing any personal problems against the backdrop of the cosmos, it becomes evident that our identities are insignificant on a cosmic scale. Most human problems stem from the ego's false identification with personal beliefs and paradigms. We are here not merely to exist but to experience the heaven that is Earth to the fullest and to play the game of transcendence until we uncover our True identity before death, becoming living evidence of the Truth in this corporeal form.

We are designed to seek and experience our version of heaven here on Earth. We, as fundamental energy fields, are reflections of the Creator, endowed with the quantum powers to co-create our own reality. Some may question this explanation of our role, but the evidence lies in those who have forgotten themselves, played the transcendental games, discovered their own Truths, and became living proof of that Truth while in this mortal coil.

Consider the Sages, Seers, and Prophets throughout history—Moses, Jesus, Mohammad, Buddha, among others. Their stories resonate because they chose to embark on the path of Truth despite the personal sacrifices and tribulations it entailed.

The Buddha, originally a prince named Siddhartha Gautama [6], was raised in luxury and shielded from the world's suffering by his father. However, his encounter with sickness, old age, and death outside the palace walls shattered his illusions. Despite his father's efforts to keep him on the path of royalty, Siddhartha renounced everything to seek Truth. His journey led him to profound realizations about the nature of existence and suffering.

In his quest for enlightenment, Siddhartha Gautama practiced extreme asceticism, enduring rigorous physical and mental disciplines. Yet, he eventually realized that such practices did not lead to liberation. Instead, sitting beneath a bodhi tree in deep meditation, Siddhartha attained enlightenment and became the Buddha, the awakened one. His teachings, encapsulated in the Four Noble Truths (Dhammacakkappavattana Sutta) [7] and the Eightfold Path (Maggavibhanga Sutta) [8], offer a path to liberation from suffering and the cycle of rebirth.

Similarly, Prophet Jesus went out into the desert and fasted for forty days and forty nights in search of his Truth. According to the Gospel of Matthew (4:1-11) [9], during this time, Prophet Jesus was tempted by the devil. The devil first tempted him, saying, "If you are the Son of God, command that these stones become loaves of bread." Prophet Jesus responded, "It is written: 'One does not live on bread alone, but on every word that comes forth from the mouth of God.'"

Then, the devil took Prophet Jesus to the holy city and made him stand on the parapet of the temple, saying, "If you are the Son of God, throw yourself down. For it is written: 'He will command his angels concerning you, and with their hands, they will support you lest you dash your foot

---

[6] https://www.worldhistory.org/Siddhartha_Gautama/

[7] https://www.accesstoinsight.org/tipitaka/sn/sn56/sn56.011.than.html

[8] https://www.accesstoinsight.org/tipitaka/sn/sn45/sn45.008.than.html

[9] https://www.biblegateway.com/passage/?search=Matthew%204%3A1-11&version=NIV

against a stone.'" Prophet Jesus answered, "Again it is written, 'You shall not put the Lord, your God, to the test.'"

Next, the devil took Prophet Jesus to a very high mountain and showed him all the kingdoms of the world in their magnificence, saying, "All these I shall give to you if you will prostrate yourself and worship me." Prophet Jesus rebuked him, saying, "Get away, Satan! It is written: 'The Lord, your God, shall you worship and him alone shall you serve.'"

Then, the devil left Prophet Jesus, and angels came and ministered to him. This profound test in the desert demonstrated Prophet Jesus' unwavering faith in God's word and his rejection of worldly temptations, affirming his commitment to his divine mission.

Prophet Jesus' life and teachings were characterized by compassion, humility, and a deep sense of spiritual truth. He preached love for one another, forgiveness, and the importance of faith. His parables and miracles illustrated profound spiritual lessons, such as the parable of the Good Samaritan and the miracle of feeding the multitude with a few loaves and fish. These acts exemplified his message of compassion and the kingdom of heaven being accessible to all who believed.

In his ministry, Prophet Jesus healed the sick, gave sight to the blind, and comforted the downtrodden. He welcomed sinners and outcasts, challenging social norms and emphasizing the value of every individual in the eyes of God. His Sermon on the Mount (Matthew 57) [10] encapsulated his teachings, offering guidance on living a righteous life, prayer, and forgiveness.

Those who choose the path of Truth have a deep sense of clarity. They stick to their path because they can feel it resonates deep within themselves. The life of Prophet Mohammed is another example of this. Born into a respected Arab tribe in Mecca, Prophet Muhammad was about 40 years old when he received his first divine revelation in a cave on Mount Hira [11]. The Quran recounts this profound moment in Surah Al-'Alaq (96:1-5) [12], where the angel Gabriel appeared to Prophet Muhammad, instructing him with the opening verses: "Read in the name of your Lord who created - Created man from a clinging substance. Read,

---

[10] https://www.biblegateway.com/passage/?search=Matthew%205-7&version=NIV
[11] https://thepilgrim.co/cave-of-hira/
[12] https://quran.com/en/al-alaq/1-5

and your Lord is the most Generous - Who taught by the pen - Taught man that which he knew not." This pivotal moment marked the beginning of his prophethood and the dissemination of Islam's monotheistic message.

Initially met with indifference and ridicule by many in Mecca, Prophet Muhammad faced significant opposition as he condemned idol worship and polytheism. His teachings threatened the established social order and economic interests tied to the annual pilgrimage to the Kaaba. The Quraysh [13], Mecca's dominant tribe and custodians of the Kaaba, viewed Prophet Muhammad's message as a direct challenge to their authority and economic prosperity.

Despite pressures to compromise or abandon his mission, Prophet Muhammad remained steadfast in his commitment to spreading the message of monotheism, compassion, and social justice. His perseverance through persecution, including boycotts, threats, and physical attacks, exemplified his unwavering dedication to God's revelation.

The Quran records numerous revelations (ayahs) that emphasize moral guidance, justice, and compassion. For instance, Surah AlMa'idah (5:8) [14]states: "O you who have believed, be persistently standing firm for Allah, witnesses in justice, and do not let the hatred of a people prevent you from being just. Be just; that is nearer to righteousness."

Prophet Muhammad's life not only serves as a model of spiritual devotion and resilience but also as a testament to the transformative power of faith and divine revelation. Through his teachings and actions, Prophet Muhammad established a community based on principles of equality, compassion, and social justice, laying the foundation for one of the world's major religions.

Today, Prophet Muhammad's legacy endures through the global

Muslim community's adherence to his teachings, known as the Sunnah, and the Quran's timeless guidance. Despite facing ridicule, persecution, and attempts to suppress his message, Mohammad remained steadfast, guided by his profound faith in the unity of God (Tawhid) and the righteousness of his mission.

---

[13] https://thepilgrim.co/bani-shaiba/

[14] https://quran.com/en/al-maidah/8

Prophet Moses, born into the Hebrew community during a time of enslavement in Egypt, initially enjoyed privilege and protection within Pharaoh's household. Raised as a prince, he was shielded from the harsh realities faced by his people. However, as he matured and became increasingly aware of the suffering of the Israelites under Egyptian oppression, Prophet Moses could no longer ignore the injustice surrounding him. Driven by a profound sense of justice and guided by his growing connection to God's presence, Prophet Moses made a pivotal decision to renounce his princely status and align himself with the plight of his enslaved kin.

In the Bible (Exodus 2:11-15) [15], Prophet Moses intervenes in a violent altercation between an Egyptian taskmaster and a Hebrew slave, ultimately resulting in the death of the taskmaster. Fearing repercussions, Prophet Moses flees Egypt and finds refuge in the land of Midian. It was during his sojourn in Midian that Prophet Moses encountered God through a burning bush on Mount Horeb (Exodus 3:1-15) [16]. From the midst of the flames, God spoke to Prophet Moses, commissioning him to return to Egypt and lead the Israelites to freedom—a daunting task that Prophet Moses initially resisted but ultimately embraced out of obedience to God's will.

Throughout the Exodus narrative, Prophet Moses faced formidable challenges: confronting the powerful Pharaoh, enduring the plagues that struck Egypt, and guiding a restless and often rebellious people through the wilderness. Despite his initial doubts and insecurities, Prophet Moses remained steadfast in his faith and commitment to God's commandments. His leadership was marked by moments of profound faith, such as when he parted the Red Sea to facilitate the Israelites' escape from pursuing Egyptian forces (Exodus 14:21-31) [17], and moments of human frailty, such as when he struck the rock in frustration instead of speaking to it as commanded (Numbers 20:712) [18].

---

[15] https://www.biblegateway.com/passage/?search=Exodus%202%3A11-15&version=NIV

[16] https://www.biblegateway.com/passage/?search=Exodus%203%3A1-15&version=NIV

[17] https://www.biblegateway.com/passage/?search=Exodus%2014%3A21-31&version=NIV

[18] https://www.biblegateway.com/passage/?search=Numbers%2020%3A712&version=

All these great prophets followed their Truth and spread the message of Oneness, the core and the only reality we are part of. Their words resonated deep within billions of people across oceans of time and space because they all connected us to the One source generally. They transcended the bounds of time and space by realizing and being true to the One Awareness who became the evidence of truth here on earth for all humanity.

They challenged the conventions of their times, speaking truth to power and embodying principles that transcended individual and societal limitations. Yet, as time passed and their teachings were institutionalized, the purity of their messages sometimes became obscured by human ego and institutional agendas. When teaching becomes enshrined in institutions, the focus often shifts from spiritual truths to organizational maintenance and power dynamics, potentially diluting the original transformative intent.

It's essential not to judge any message or signpost, as they are inherently beautiful until institutionalized. Once institutionalized, the institution often overshadows the message itself, allowing the human ego and false identities to obscure the fundamental truths originally conveyed.

Some may perceive suffering as integral to transcendence, yet it's crucial to recognize that transcendent experiences can be effortless if we avoid being deceived by our minds and personal identities. These revered figures in history endured profound suffering within their human identities until they discovered the Truth.

Consider the profound idea that figures such as Prophet Mohammad, Jesus, Moses, and the religions of Abraham couldn't fully reveal the Truth and reality, because humanity wasn't yet ready to grasp it. At that time, the intellectual and spiritual maturity required to understand such deep concepts wasn't prevalent. Hence, these great figures shaped their teachings into methodologies that their contemporaries could comprehend and relate to.

Qabalah in Judaism: Qabalah, or Kabbalah, is an esoteric method, discipline, and school of thought in Jewish mysticism. Originating in the 12th to 13th centuries, Qabalah explores the nature of God, the universe, and the human soul. It delves into concepts such as the Tree of Life,

---

NIV

which maps the spiritual journey through ten interconnected sephirot (spheres), each representing aspects of God's nature and the human experience. By engaging with these teachings, adherents seek to achieve spiritual enlightenment and a deeper understanding of divine truths.

Gnostic Christianity: Gnostic Christianity emerged in the early centuries of the Christian era, emphasizing knowledge (gnosis) as the path to salvation. Gnostics believed that the material world was created by a lesser divine being and that true salvation came through esoteric knowledge of the divine realm. Central to Gnostic teachings is the idea of the divine spark within each person, which can be awakened through inner knowledge and enlightenment. Gnostic texts, like the Gospel of Thomas, offer alternative views on Jesus's teachings, focusing on personal spiritual awakening rather than institutionalized religion.

Sufism in Islam: Sufism is the mystical branch of Islam, focusing on the inward search for God and the personal experience of the divine. Sufis believe in a direct, personal relationship with God, achieved through practices like dhikr (remembrance of God), meditation, and poetry. Figures such as Rumi, Shams Tabriz, Ibn Sina (Avicenna), and Mansur al-Hallaj are revered within Sufism for their profound spiritual insights and contributions. Rumi's poetry, for example, encapsulates the soul's longing for union with the divine, while alHallaj's declaration of "Ana al-Haqq" (I am the Truth) reflects the ultimate Sufi experience of merging with God.

Each of these mystical traditions within Abrahamic religions offers deeper, often esoteric interpretations of their faiths, suggesting that the ultimate truths might have been too complex or advanced for the general populace to understand at the time. As humanity evolves spiritually, these deeper teachings provide a path to greater understanding and enlightenment.

Prophets like Moses, Jesus, and Muhammad likely understood far more about the ultimate Truth than what they revealed in their holy texts. They recognized that the people of their time weren't ready to grasp the profound depths of spiritual reality, so they adapted their teachings to match the society's level of understanding, using parables and simple lessons. For a smaller group who had transcended the false identities of body and mind, they introduced deeper, esoteric teachings— like Qabalah in Judaism, Gnostic Christianity, and Sufism in Islam. These mystical paths delve into the hidden layers of existence, guiding individuals toward direct experiences of the divine. By planting these seeds, the prophets ensured that as humanity evolved, those ready to embrace deeper mysteries could awaken to their true nature as pure Awareness.

Imagine life as a grand movie, and you, the actor, are cast in various roles, each one grappling with different experiences like hunger, pain, and poverty. While these roles can be intense and demanding, deep down, you know they are temporary and fleeting, merely scenes in a great story. The suffering belongs to the character, but as the actor, you find joy and fulfillment in playing the part. The real challenge arises when you forget your identity as the actor and become solely identified with the character you are portraying.

You are, in essence, True Awareness, cognizant of your mind, body, and ego navigating this brief and contrasting earthly existence. To truly awaken, it's akin to experiencing a death before dying— shedding all illusions about who you think you are and remaining anchored in pure Awareness. This state of pure Awareness is detached from the transient experiences of the body, mind, ego, and worldly possessions.

Life's transcendent games continuously test your identity against a backdrop of distractions and challenges—unrealistic demands, personal desires, fears, and temptations. It's not a matter of passing or failing these tests but about maintaining your transcendent identity amidst the trials. Each moment serves as an opportunity to reinforce your understanding and connection to your True Self.

Daily, like an audience member watching a movie, you observe the inner drama unfold—ego-centric thoughts, fears, desires, and the relentless chatter of the mind. Through practice, you learn to observe these occurrences without identification, recognizing yourself as the detached witness of this inner world.

Embracing this understanding, I once practiced feeling and affirming my emptiness, akin to a newborn infant within the conditioned limits of my body, mind, and personality. This practice proved immensely liberating and transformative.

Awakening to your own truth requires questioning everything, cultivating curiosity, and engaging in self-inquiry. Through meditation and self-reflection, you may uncover new perspectives and inner peace, aligning with your true essence.

If the calling within you is absent, heed your inner guidance. This path is not for those facing psychological challenges or deeply entrenched in ego identification. Liberation from mental and psychological suffering through self-realization demands readiness and inner longing. My own journey began with an unexpected self-help book, "Think and Grow Rich" by Napoleon Hill [19], despite its initial irrelevance to my spiritual calling.

In the beginning, I had no idea that what I was longing for was within me. I wandered, seeking it in external riches, food, gambling, alcohol, vanity—all the sensory stimulations that captivate our attention. Yet, the "within" I sought wasn't within my physical body or organs but a state of emptiness, meditation, and connection to the field of awareness beyond identity and conceptual frameworks.

Dr. Wayne Dyer's parable [20] has always resonated deeply with me: "The story of the man who dropped his keys in his living room during a power failure. The man groped around on the floor in the darkness for a long time and couldn't find his keys. Then he noticed that way down the block, a streetlight was on! So, he left his house, went down the street, and started looking for his keys under the streetlight. After a while, his neighbor saw him and went over to see if he could help.

'What's wrong?'

'I dropped my keys.'

'Where did you drop them?'

'In my living room.'

'Then why are you looking for them under this streetlight?'

'Because the light's so much better out here!'"

Dr. Wayne Dyer's parable powerfully illustrates how we often search for answers and fulfillment outside ourselves, where it's more comfortable or where the light seems brighter, instead of within the depths of our own

---

[19] https://www.goodreads.com/book/show/30186948-think-and-grow-rich
[20] https://www.listennotes.com/podcasts/prosperity-practice/a-parable-by-wayne-dyer-keyscPeE1VrBqsU/#google_vignette

being. The journey to self-realization often begins when we realize that the keys to our true fulfillment and understanding lie within our own hearts and minds, beyond the allure of external distractions.

Chapter 6

Emerging from Shadows

"The wound is the place where the Light enters you." —

Rumi

It all began with the great recession of 2008—a seismic shift that upended my world overnight. My business, once thriving and full of promises, began to crumble under the weight of an economy in freefall. The stability I had worked so hard to build evaporated, and I found myself standing at the edge of a precipice with no safety net in sight.

Desperate to navigate these tumultuous waters, with overwhelming amount stress and anxiety I thought I needed a break. I placed my trust in someone I thought was a friend and a loyal business partner. I handed over the reins of my business, the keys to my assets, even the combinations to my safes filled with most of my savings. In a move that still echoes in my memory like a bad dream, he betrayed me, taking everything and leaving me with nothing but empty accounts and shattered trust. He seized the business we built together, emptied my safes, claimed properties, and destroyed our partnership without so much as a thank you or acknowledgment for the knowledge and opportunities I'd shared with him.

The years that followed were some of the darkest I'd ever known. I was thrust into a life of poverty, desperation, and despair. Every day there was a battle against the crushing weight of a victim mentality that threatened to consume me. I felt broken—not just financially, but emotionally, physically, and spiritually. The person I thought I was had been stripped away, leaving me raw and vulnerable.

For nearly two years, I grappled with unemployment, watching helplessly as my last savings dwindled to nothing. The fear and uncertainty were overwhelming; it was as if I was trapped in a nightmare from which I couldn't wake up. I had always envisioned a certain path for my life, but now that path had been obliterated, and I was lost in uncharted territory.

But in the depths of this darkness, a subtle shift began to occur. Faced with the rubble of my former life, I started to question everything I thought I knew about myself. My ego and personal identity, those constructs I had believed were me, composed of my body, personality, thoughts, and beliefs—began to reveal themselves as illusions. They were merely roles I had been playing, masks I had been wearing in the grand play of life.

Through the practice of mindfulness and awareness, I discovered a new way of seeing. I learned to observe my pain without becoming it, to witness my thoughts without being controlled by them. This shift in perspective was like a breath of fresh air in a suffocating room. I realized that the hardships I faced were not just random punishments from a cruel universe but opportunities to learn, grow, and evolve into a better version of myself.

Forgiveness became a powerful tool on this journey. I found the strength to forgive my former business partner, not for his sake, but for mine. Holding onto anger and resentment was like carrying a burning coal, hoping it would harm him while it only burned me. Letting go of that weight allowed me to reclaim my power and move forward.

Every obstacle I came to see was a steppingstone in the transcendence game of life. These challenges tested my true identity against the distractions and illusions of the world—material loss, betrayal, fear, and the temptation to give up. But they also offered invaluable lessons about resilience, self-awareness, and the impermanent nature of our circumstances.

Looking back now, I understand that life had other plans for me— plans that required me to shed the layers of who I thought I was to discover who I truly am. The collapse of my external world forced me to embark on an internal journey, one that led me to depths I never knew existed. It was a rebirth of sorts, a dying before death, where I let go of illusions and embraced the essence of my being.

Today, I stand not as a victim of my past but as a testament to the transformative power of adversity. The financial ruin, the betrayal, the years of despair—they were all catalysts that propelled me toward awakening. They taught me that while we cannot always control the events that happen to us, we can choose how we respond to them. We can allow them to break us down or use them to build ourselves up.

In embracing mindfulness and awareness, I found a path to healing and empowerment. I learned that true stability comes not from external possessions or identities but from an unshakable connection to the core of our being. Life's challenges continue, as they always will, but now I face them with a sense of peace and a knowing that every experience is an opportunity for growth.

"In the end, we will remember not the words of our enemies, but the silence of our friends." –

Martin Luther King Jr.

During this tough period, most people turned away, unable to grasp what we were going through. But my younger sister and her husband stood by us, giving us the emotional support we needed.

"True friends are those who stand by you in your darkest moments because they are willing to brave the shadows with you."

We learn profound lessons in the depths of adversity about resilience and the importance of those who stand with us. They are not just supporters but pillars of strength, showing us the power of human connection in overcoming life's trials. Their presence teaches us that true support transcends words—it's about being there, unwavering, through the darkest of times. They embody the lesson that our strength is often magnified in the company of those who believe in us and stand by us when everything else feels uncertain.

Out of fear of losing everything, I made a risky decision to buy a restaurant. It drained us—physically, emotionally, and financially. While managing the restaurant, I took my son to Pismo Beach for his birthday, and there, I broke my collarbone. This added physical pain to our already difficult situation.

Every day was a struggle. I worry constantly about my health, money, and mental well-being. I counted every dollar to make sure we could pay our bills. It was hard and humiliating to be in my forties and struggle to make ends meet.

Amid all this, I searched desperately for answers. Why was I facing so much hardship after a period of relative ease? I asked God repeatedly, "Why me? Why are you testing me like this?" I didn't understand it then, but looking back now, over ten years later, I realized those difficult times were teaching me important lessons. They forced me to look inside myself and think deeply about my life's purpose.

I learned that personal struggles are not punishments but opportunities for growth. They're like nightmares that wake us up from a bad dream. Those tough years pushed me to discover inner strength and resilience that I didn't know I had. They stripped away the superficial parts of my identity and showed me what really matters.

"Out of suffering have emerged the strongest souls; the most massive characters are seared with scars." –

Khalil Gibran.

During that unforgettable period, I faced the harsh realities of financial struggle day in and day out, uncertain if I could make ends meet as each month drew to a close. Hitting rock bottom was a profound test that left me questioning how I would deal with such challenging times. In those moments, it was just me and my wife, and I owe her everything for being my unwavering support.

My wife stood by me like a steadfast oak tree, providing the strength and support that held us together when I felt most vulnerable. Her presence was a pillar of stability amidst the uncertainty, her belief in us never wavering even in our darkest hours. She didn't just weather the storm beside me; she stood tall against its fiercest winds, offering me courage and resilience when my own faltered.

In those moments of adversity, her love and support were my guiding light. She reminded me that I wasn't alone in facing life's challenges. Her unconditional faith in our journey and her steadfast commitment taught me profound lessons about resilience and the power of partnership.

"A good wife is a reflection of a successful man, and behind every successful man, there is a strong woman."

My wife, Gitti, epitomized strength in every aspect, surpassing me in ways I couldn't have imagined. Without her unwavering support, I doubt I would be here today. She isn't just a remarkable wife; she's an exceptional mother who raised our two bright and handsome boys. Having a strong life partner like her, who understands empathetically without holding resentments, is invaluable.

Gitti's strength wasn't just a façade; it was a pillar that held our family together during our darkest times. She tackled every challenge with a resilience that would put most men to shame, supporting me mentally, emotionally, physically, and even financially. Her days began before the sun rose, rushing to the restaurant to prepare and cook fresh dishes, ensuring the smooth operation of our business. She seamlessly transitioned to managing the front of the restaurant, greeting customers with a smile that masked the exhaustion she felt.

By mid-afternoon, Gitti hurried home to attend to our boys, ensuring they were fed and safely back from school. Despite the whirlwind of our daily lives, she never missed a beat. By late afternoon, she was back at the restaurant, preparing for the evening rush, orchestrating the chaos with a grace that belied the strain she endured. She returned home well past bedtime, only to rise before dawn and repeat the cycle, day after relentless day.

She became the glue that bound us together as a family, her perseverance a beacon of hope during our darkest moments. I can't overstate the credit she deserves for her unwavering courage, hope, and unwavering belief that we would not only survive but thrive. In the quiet of the night, when anxiety threatened to overwhelm me, Gitti's presence was a calming force. Sometimes, I would wake in the early hours, struggling to catch my breath, finding solace only in the cool darkness of our neighborhood streets. The burden was immense, emotionally and psychologically, yet Gitti's steadfast support provided a lifeline that kept me going day by day.

Her dedication wasn't just to our family's survival; it was a testament to the power of love and commitment in overcoming adversity. Through her tireless efforts and unwavering belief in our future, Gitti taught me invaluable lessons about resilience, strength, and the boundless capacity of the human spirit. She embodied the essence of partnership, standing beside me not just in good times but especially when life tested us most harshly.

When it became just too much to bear, I found myself venting to my brother-in-law, pouring out my grievances about the unfairness of life and my string of misfortunes. His response was simple yet profound: "What can you do about it now? The past is just a memory; it doesn't exist anymore. There's no need to keep reliving your misfortunes."

"What can I do?" I replied, feeling frustrated. "I'm doing everything I can, but it's not enough."

"Exactly," he said calmly. "isn't it time to surrender everything to your Creator? The One who created this vast universe and life itself."

His words lingered with me. One morning, as I stood in the shower, I made a conscious decision to wash away all the negativity that had consumed me — mentally, emotionally, physically, and spiritually. From that moment on, I resolved to remain present. To aid me in this journey, I developed tools to keep my mind grounded in the now. Meditation walks in nature, swimming in cold water, the soothing warmth of a hot shower, bouncing on a trampoline, writing, playing chess, cards, or pool, listening to audiobooks or music — and above all, connecting deeply with my wife — became my anchors.

These practices weren't easy; they took years of dedication and perfecting. But gradually, they helped me cultivate a sense of presence in every moment, teaching me that true peace lies in embracing the present rather than dwelling on the past or worrying about the future.

In Islamic tradition, the story of Prophet Muhammad's night journey and ascension (Isra and Mi'raj) is significant. During a period of persecution in Mecca, Muhammad faced immense hardships as he preached monotheism and social justice. His followers endured boycotts, torture, and exile. Despite these challenges, Muhammad remained steadfast in his faith and mission. One night, guided by the archangel Gabriel, Muhammad journeyed from Mecca to Jerusalem and ascended through the seven heavens, meeting various prophets along the way. This miraculous journey affirmed Muhammad's prophethood and strengthened his resolve to spread the message of Islam. His endurance through trials exemplifies the importance of faith, perseverance, and trust in divine guidance.

In the Bible, the story of Job stands out as a profound example of suffering and resilience. Job, a righteous man in the land of Uz, faces unimaginable trials. He loses his wealth, his health deteriorates, and his children perish in a series of calamities. Despite his suffering, Job maintains his faith and integrity, refusing to curse God. His friends argue that his suffering must be a punishment for sin, but Job insists on his innocence and demands answers from God. Through his ordeal, Job undergoes a transformative journey of self-discovery and spiritual growth.

In the end, God restores Job's fortunes and blesses him with even greater prosperity, reaffirming Job's faith and demonstrating the mysterious ways of divine providence.

In Buddhism, the story of Siddhartha Gautama, who later became known as the Buddha, illustrates the path of suffering and enlightenment. Born into luxury as a prince, Siddhartha was shielded from the realities of human suffering. One day, he ventured beyond the palace walls and encountered old age, sickness, and death. Deeply moved by these encounters, Siddhartha renounced his princely life in search of spiritual awakening. He practiced severe asceticism for years but realized that extreme deprivation did not lead to enlightenment. Finally, under the Bodhi tree, Siddhartha attained profound insight into the nature of suffering and the path to liberation. He became the Buddha, the awakened one, teaching the Four Noble Truths and the Eightfold Path to help others transcend suffering and achieve enlightenment.

From Hinduism, the story of Lord Krishna imparting the Bhagavad Gita to Arjuna on the battlefield of Kurukshetra provides profound insights into the nature of suffering and duty. Arjuna, a skilled warrior and prince, faces a moral crisis on the eve of battle against his own relatives and teachers. Overwhelmed by grief and doubt, Arjuna turns to Krishna, his charioteer and divine guide, for counsel. Krishna imparts spiritual wisdom through the Bhagavad Gita, teaching Arjuna about the eternal soul, the impermanence of the physical body, and the importance of righteous action (dharma). Through their dialogue, Krishna encourages Arjuna to fulfill his duty as a warrior with detachment and devotion to the divine. Arjuna embraces his role, recognizing the necessity of facing challenges with courage and moral clarity.

Across these diverse traditions, the stories of prophets and spiritual figures emphasize that suffering, while inevitable, catalyzes personal growth, spiritual awakening, and a deeper connection with the divine. Just as these spiritual journeys require traversing realms beyond mere physical existence, so too does our understanding of energy and potential in our lives.

Always remember!

- Suffering challenges, us to confront our deepest fears and limitations.
- It strips away superficial identities and reveals our inner strength.

- Through suffering, we learn compassion for ourselves and others.

You can have energy or electricity running in your walls, but that does not mean you can watch TV, play video games, listen to audio devices, cook a meal, have a cold drink, wash or dry your clothes by machine, charge your phone, turn on the lights, use the Wi-Fi, and so on without getting devices for each function and plug it to the wall first. In the same way, there are many dimensions, fields of energy, and powers that are beyond the reach and comprehension of humanity until we transcend our limited physicality and connect with them in our quantum state.

In our journey through life, we often encounter challenges that test our resolve and push us to our limits. These struggles may appear daunting and impossible, yet they serve a profound purpose in shaping our character and fostering inner strength. Just as a seed must push through the darkness of the soil to reach the sunlight, so too do we grow through adversity. Like the butterfly's struggle to emerge from its cocoon, these adversities are necessary for our growth.

"A man found a cocoon of a butterfly. One day, a small opening appeared. He sat and watched the butterfly for several hours as it struggled to force its body through that little hole.

Then, it seemed to stop making progress. It appeared as if it had gotten as far as it could, and it could go no further. So, the man decided to help the butterfly. He took a pair of scissors and snipped off the remaining bit of the cocoon. The butterfly then emerged easily, but it had a swollen body and small, shriveled wings.

The man continued to watch the butterfly because he expected that, at any moment, the wings would enlarge and expand to be able to support the body, which would contract in time.

Neither happened! In fact, the butterfly spent the rest of its life crawling around with a swollen body and shriveled wings. It never was able to fly."

The story of the butterfly teaches us that without the struggle to break free, its wings would remain weak and incapable of flight. Similarly, each obstacle we face presents an opportunity for transformation and renewal, teaching us valuable lessons about resilience and the power of perseverance. It is in these moments of struggle that we discover our true capabilities and unearth hidden potential that propel us forward on our path of self-discovery and spiritual evolution.

Embracing this journey may seem challenging at first, but with belief, focused attention, and guidance, everything becomes possible.

By shedding old beliefs, conditioning, false identities, and the subconscious mind, we pave the way to reprogram our conscious and subconscious with a new, authentic paradigm. While I cannot walk this path for you, I am here to offer support and guidance. With sincere belief, self-inquiry, and unwavering focus, you will attain clarity of self and truth, transcending limitations and embracing your fullest potential.

Chapter 7

Nothing Like the Present

"The more you are focused on time—past and future—the more you miss the Now, the most precious thing there is." –

Eckhart Tolle

Being present is the key to experiencing true life. The past and future are illusions created by our minds, often distracting us from the now. These illusions, fueled by memory and imagination, shape our perception but can lead us away from living fully in the present moment.

Only Now is true; everything else, including time, past, and future, are illusions of the mind. The biggest players in this illusion are memory and imagination. While these faculties can be useful, they can also be detrimental if misused. Memory allows us to learn from past experiences, and imagination enables us to plan and dream. However, when overemphasized, they can trap us in a cycle of regret and anxiety. Everything is happening spontaneously in the present moment, and when this moment is over, that's the end of it. You cannot be in the past or future; you can only be in the now. You can imagine a beautiful or ugly future, you can reminisce about a wonderful memory or an ugly past, but you can only be in the now. Nothing else matters and cannot be experienced except for now.

Ask any animal in the wild what time it is, and they will laugh at your question. All species except humans are present, spontaneously letting life happen for them and around them. Humans are always busy preparing to live, always getting ready for the next—from kindergarten to school, to higher education, to career, to retirement, all the way to death, and even ready for after death. Become present and aware of now, surrender to all the happenings for you and around you, and let life happen because you are alive at this moment only.

Become spontaneous to be more stable and peaceful at whatever you are doing, whether it is school, work, fun, or play. It takes practice because the mind will attack over and over to take you on a journey to the past and future. Don't judge your thoughts and mind; instead, become aware of your attention so you can shift your attention to your presence.

"We are very good at preparing to live, but not very good at living. We know how to sacrifice ten years for a diploma, and we are willing to work very hard to get a job, a car, a house, and so on. But we have difficulty remembering that we are alive in the present moment, the only moment there is for us to be alive." —

Thich Nhat Hanh

The psychological mind likes to linger on the past and duel with the future. The mind loves creating victimization of the past and a worryfilled future. When the mind creates victimization, practicing mindfulness exercises or cognitive-behavioral techniques can help shift focus. The mind can't stay present in the now because it finds the Now boring, out of the habit of always doing something, always getting ready for what's next. So, the psychological mind loves creating little stories about the past and future. Most of the narratives are not even real. The mind functions to give the sense of continuity to attract the consciousness to stay attached and identify as the body and mind.

The mind acts as it's subconscious programming, playing the habitual program by genetic memory. Our genes remember the memory of the cavemen who were hunting and gathering most of the time, and while resting, always remembered the worst memories and used imagination to create worst-case scenarios to be able to survive lion or tiger attacks or worse. So, the mind is genetically programmed to remember the worst memories and use the imagination to recreate the worst scenarios to be able to survive any circumstance.

Freud suggested that much of our behavior is influenced by the unconscious mind, which holds onto primitive instincts and fears. The unconscious mind operates outside of our conscious awareness and stores our deepest thoughts, memories, and desires. Freud's concept of the unconscious mind highlights how our behaviors and emotions are often driven by these hidden elements, which include repressed memories and unresolved conflicts from our past. These primitive instincts and fears, remnants of our early human ancestors, continue to influence our behavior and reactions, often without us realizing it. By becoming aware of these unconscious influences, we can start to transcend them and live more fully in the present.

We don't live in the cavemen era, so it is time to transcend this old programming. We can do this by becoming aware of the thoughts of the ugly past and the imagination of a worrisome future.

"There are only two days in the year that nothing can be done. One is called yesterday, and the other is called tomorrow, so today is the right day to love, believe, do, and mostly live." —

Dalai Lama

You cannot do anything yesterday and tomorrow; it is best to invest all your energy in today. The sense of continuity comes from the past and future. Take out my memory and imagination, and that's the end of the sense of continuity. Anything time-related disappears when the sense of continuity doesn't exist. Therefore, time, past, and future are just constructs of the mind and have no real power. All the power exists in the Now; that is the real freedom from my mind's illusion. All psychological, emotional, and mental problems from my past and future disappear when I stay present and aware of the Now.

Please don't misunderstand me when I say stay present, so your problems go away. I know from experience that with the power of now, you can experience peace, joy, happiness, and contentment. The psychological, emotional, and mental problems don't disappear by staying present in the now, but your focus of attention, which gives them more power, is taken away from them. Anytime you put your focus of attention on something, you give it the power to become stronger.

I define the focus of my attention as a flashlight on a blackboard full of the following writings:

- **Love:** A profound and selfless affection towards others, often involving care, concern, and compassion.

- **Passion:** Intense enthusiasm or fervor for something or someone, driving creativity and dedication.

- **Compassion:** Deep empathy and a desire to help others in distress, reflecting kindness and understanding.

- **Hate:** A strong aversion or intense dislike that can consume thoughts and lead to negative actions.

- **Anger:** A powerful emotion of displeasure or hostility, often a response to perceived wrongs.

- **Jealousy:** A feeling of envy towards someone's advantages, successes, or possessions, coupled with insecurity.

- **Resentment:** Lingering bitterness or indignation from past wrongs or mistreatment.

- **Hope:** The optimistic expectation and desire for positive outcomes in the future.

- **Pride:** A sense of satisfaction and self-respect stemming from one's achievements or qualities.

- **Fear:** An emotional response to perceived threats, leading to anxiety and caution.

- **Worry:** Persistent concern or anxiety about potential problems or uncertainties.

- **Anxiety:** A state of unease and apprehension about future uncertainties or challenges.

- **Indignation:** Righteous anger or annoyance provoked by unfair treatment or injustice.

- **Envy:** A feeling of discontentment and desire aroused by someone else's possessions, qualities, or luck.

- **Suffering:** The experience of physical or emotional pain and distress.

- **Pain:** A distressing sensation often caused by injury, illness, or emotional turmoil.

- **Impatience:** Restlessness and frustration stemming from a lack of tolerance for delays or opposition.

- **Joy:** A feeling of great pleasure and happiness, often accompanied by a sense of contentment.

- **Happiness:** A state of well-being and satisfaction, characterized by positive emotions and fulfillment.

- **Care:** Concern and consideration for others, often manifesting in protective and nurturing actions.

- **Grief:** Deep sorrow and anguish, especially after losing someone or something significant.

- **Despair:** A profound loss of hope and a feeling of utter helplessness.

- **Guilt:** A sense of remorse and responsibility for actions that one perceives as wrong or harmful.

- **Helplessness:** A feeling of powerlessness and inability to influence or change one's circumstances.

- **Patience:** The capacity to accept delays, difficulties, or discomfort without getting angry or upset.

- **Shyness:** The feeling of being reserved or timid in social situations, often due to self-consciousness.

- **Modesty:** Humility and a lack of arrogance, often involving a downplaying of one's abilities or achievements.

- **Imagination:** The ability to form new ideas and concepts that are not present to the senses, fostering creativity and innovation.

- **Memory:** The mental capacity to store, retain, and recall information and past experiences.

- **Feelings:** Emotional states or reactions that are often subjective and can influence thoughts and behaviors.

- **Emotions:** Complex reactions that involve physiological responses, feelings, and thoughts, affecting our mood and behavior.

And much more: Countless other thoughts and emotions that color our perception and experience of life.

I give life to any of these words by focusing my flashlight on them; otherwise, they are a bunch of meaningless rubbish on the board and have no power over me. I give them power by putting the focus of my attention on them. I have developed systems and tools to get my attention off useless things and focus on positive things to stay present in the now. Some of these tools are not universal, and everyone should find and develop their own tools to stay present in the Now.

Since everyone is different, everyone's interest varies as well. Everything that attracts you is not a bad habit, but from a mindful place, ask your heart what is most attractive to you that can pull your attention immediately. Like jumping in cold water immediately attracts all my attention to my presence, no matter where I am mentally, emotionally, or psychologically.

Thoughts of the past and future come and go in my mind daily. The less I pay attention to them, the less they have power over me and control me. If I remain identified as my personal individual ego, tempted with thoughts and interested in it, then it has the power to pull me like a dog on a leash in every direction it chooses. Knowing that I am not the individual person and remaining the witness of my awareness, I hold my power and refuse to be a puppet of my mind, feelings, emotions, thoughts, past, and future.

By staying present, you are taking the source of energy from the mind, feelings, emotions, past, and future. A lighter will be functional if it has lighter fluid in it; the minute you take away the lighter fluid, the lighter becomes useless. The moon seems to be shining its own light, but it's obvious it has no light or power of shining on its own without light from the sun. A house powered by electricity can give you so many comforts like a refrigerator, water heater, stove, TV, radio, WiFi, and much more. None of these appliances would be useful if the electricity running through the walls to the outlet is cut off.

The electricity, lighter fluid, and the reflection of sunlight are akin to the focus of my conscious attention, which powers the mind to create thoughts about the past and future. Just as electricity energizes household appliances, lighter fluid fuels a flame, and sunlight illuminates the moon, my conscious attention gives energy to the mind. This energy allows the mind to wander, weaving a tapestry of thoughts, memories, and anticipations that pull me away from the present moment. By withdrawing this power, I can prevent the mind from spinning its web of past regrets and future anxieties.

When I choose not to energize the mind, I naturally remain present in the now—a state of peace, joy, tranquility, and contentment. The power of the now lies in its state of "unhappening." In this state, everything flows effortlessly, free from the interference of the mind. The present moment becomes a sanctuary where the pure essence of being can be experienced.

This state of unhappening is a profound realization: peace and contentment are not goals to be achieved but inherent aspects of our natural state. When the mind's influence diminishes, these qualities reveal themselves effortlessly, reminding us that the present is not something to conquer—it is simply to be lived.

Yes, the wind is blowing, the cars are driving, clouds are passing, trees are swirling, birds are singing, and life is happening, but I am not doing anything except witnessing. Being a present witness to all the happenings in now allows me to engage with life fully without being entangled in it. This state of witnessing is an active engagement with the world, where I observe and appreciate the flow of life without becoming attached to any particular outcome. It's like watching a river flow: I see the water moving, I hear its sound, but I remain on the bank, untouched by its current.

By consciously choosing to witness life rather than being swept away by it, I cultivate a sense of detachment that brings clarity and serenity. This detachment doesn't mean disinterest or apathy; rather, it's a profound engagement with life where I am fully aware and present, yet not overwhelmed by it. This balance of engagement and detachment allows me to experience the richness of life while maintaining inner peace.

That's why I have a set of tools that I use to keep me present in the now. Whenever my mind lingers to the past or future, I use my tools to bring my attention to focus on the now. These tools are simple yet powerful reminders that anchor me to the present moment. They are not escape mechanisms but pathways to deeper awareness and presence.

As I mentioned before, some of my tools are walking in nature, swimming in cold water, hot showers, writing, reading, playing chess, and playing cards. Each of these activities helps ground me in the now, offering a tactile and sensory experience that pulls me back from the abstract realms of thought. These tools have no power to keep me content, but the power of contentment is in staying in the now. When I engage in these activities, I immerse myself fully, allowing the present moment to unfold in its entirety. This immersion is where true contentment lies, not in the activities themselves but in the state of being they facilitate.

"Living in the moment means letting go of the past and not waiting for the future. It means living your life consciously, aware that each moment you breathe is a gift." —

Oprah Winfrey

By staying in the now, I can disable the mind's function of attracting my attention to the past or future. When the mind can't steal or attract my attention anymore, then it has no power of its own to create or manipulate the past and future. It loses its ability to create drama and psychological, emotional, and mental problems. The mind remains dormant the same way the moon borrows the light from the sun, and without the reflection from the sun, it looks dead without power.

As we explore the essence of living in the present moment, it's valuable to reflect on the story of "The Monkey and the Moon." This tale beautifully encapsulates the concept of perception and the nature of our mind's reflections. Just as the monkey learns from the wise owl about the moon's true nature, understanding the role of our thoughts and consciousness helps us grasp the power of now.

"Once upon a time, in a dense, ancient forest, lived a mischievous monkey named Chatter. Chatter was renowned for his incessant chatter, his mind a whirlwind of thoughts about the past and the future. He'd often recount tales of heroic ancestors or weave elaborate fantasies of future conquests.

One serene evening, as the golden sun dipped below the horizon, casting long shadows, Chatter sat on a high branch, lost in his mental world. Suddenly, a wise old owl hooted softly. Intrigued, Chatter looked up.

"Young monkey," the owl began, "do you see the moon?"

Chatter squinted, his mind racing. "Of course, I see the moon. It's a big, round, shiny thing in the sky."

"But what do you truly see?" the owl asked.

Chatter was puzzled. "What do you mean? I see the moon."

"No, young one," the owl replied patiently. "You see the reflection of the sun on the moon. The moon itself doesn't produce light. It merely reflects."

Chatter pondered this. "So, the moon is not what it seems?"

"Exactly," the owl affirmed. "It's a mirror, reflecting something else."

"And what about me?" Chatter asked, curiosity piqued. "Am I like the moon?"

"In a way," the owl replied. "Your mind is like the moon, reflecting thoughts and emotions. But the true you, the essence of your being, is like the sun, a constant source of light and warmth."

Chatter was silent for a long moment. He realized that his constant chatter was like clouds obscuring the sun, preventing him from experiencing his true nature.

From that night on, Chatter began a journey of self-discovery. He learned to observe his thoughts without judgment, like watching clouds pass by. Gradually, the chatter subsided, and a profound

sense of peace emerged. He discovered that true happiness wasn't in the past or the future, but in the present moment, just like the moon shining brightly in the night sky.

The owl had shown Chatter the path to the power of now—to be present, to be aware, and to find peace within."

This story illustrates the lesson of staying present and letting go of the mind's endless chatter. Like Chatter, we, too, can find peace and clarity by recognizing that our thoughts and emotions are merely reflections and not the essence of who we are. The true power lies in the now, in being fully present and aware, allowing us to experience life in its purest form. By practicing mindfulness and using our personal tools, we can remain anchored in the present moment, transcending the illusions of the past and future.

Chapter 8

The Blueprint of Manifestation

"Whatever the mind can conceive and believe, it can achieve."

Napoleon Hill.

The Universe has granted all beings the power of co-creation to manifest like the creator from a place of abundance and wholeness, not from lack, desperation, pity, greed, discomfort, or weakness. Unfortunately, our society, culture, and education system have failed to nurture our belief in our own gift and power of manifestation. The more we focus our attention and believe in our limitations, the less we can manifest.

The power of manifestation is impartial; it neither discriminates nor judges desires as good or bad. The intensity of our emotions—be it passion, fear, or desire—determines how quickly we manifest outcomes. Interestingly, fear often manifests faster than desire because its emotions are raw, immediate, and unfiltered. Unlike desires, fears are usually released instantly when they arise, free from the mind's resistance, allowing them to manifest without friction.

When you deeply desire something and pray for it with all your heart, you must guard against letting your mind interfere with doubts or hopelessness. The mind, rooted in insecurities and a sense of lack, questions where, when, and how your desire will come true. This mental resistance creates friction, blocking the manifestation process.

For years, while struggling financially, I prayed, daydreamed, and created dream boards filled with images of fancy cars, luxurious villas, and private jets. I desperately wanted to manifest wealth. Yet, every time I prayed or visualized, my mind would creep in, reminding me of my struggles and reinforcing my feelings of pain and hopelessness. These negative thoughts became barriers to manifestation, despite my relentless attempts to think positively.

Manifestation requires more than just positive thinking. True manifestation happens when thought and emotion merge into a burning desire, which you then release with the gratitude of already having received it. Over time, I realized that what I was searching for wasn't in external possessions but had always been within me: the clarity of knowing the Truth. When I turned inward, I began manifesting not material wealth, but a transparent understanding of my purpose and reality.

To manifest effectively, we must learn to speak the universal language of emotion rather than relying solely on words. While the word "love" varies across languages, its emotional essence is universal. This same principle applies to manifestation: emotions and feelings—whether of love, abundance, or gratitude—transcend race, culture, religion, or any external factor.

To align with what we desire, we must feel it deeply in our hearts, radiating exuberant emotions as if we already possess it. By becoming the frequency or vibration of what we want, we open the path for the universe to bring it to us. Only then, in a state of gratitude and detachment, can we release the desire and trust that the universe will match our frequency and fulfill it effortlessly.

Gregg Braden *says, "Feel as if your prayer has already been answered!"*

Verse 106 in the Lost Gospel of Thomas says, *"When you make the two (thought and emotion) as one, you will say to the mountain, 'move away,' and the mountain will move away!"* Marry thought and emotion. Use your voice and the power of your heart when you pray!

During the dream state, I am more lucid, sleeping but very aware of my dreams and even in control of them. If I do not like my dream, I change it as easily as changing the TV channel. With enough practice, I have gained the power to choose and change my dreams as I wish. In my dream, I have the power of God to manifest as I wish, so I must manifest from abundance, from a place of wholeness and worthiness, not from disappointment, lack, desperation, or limitation.

Sometimes, during my waking state, I feel like I oversee this life, and I should change the channel and live life to my liking as I practice in my dreams. The illusions of my life, ego, identity, and personality are manifestations of my beliefs. Since my manifested reality is produced by my limited, subconscious mind, conditioning, and beliefs, then I could live a better life than what my limited and conditioned mind manifests.

I changed my reality, beliefs, and conditioned lies (imprinted in my subconscious mind in my childhood) that I am a human being living a personal egoistic life to *"We are not human beings having a spiritual experience. We are spiritual beings having a human experience,"* as said by the French philosopher, Pierre Teilhard de Chardin.

As human beings, we are identifying with one percent of what we are and ignoring ninety-nine percent of what we really are – spiritual beings. It would be surprising if Superman knowingly chose to identify as Clark Kent (his human character) rather than identifying as Superman. What if, because of his false identification, he believed he had no superpowers when he had them all along?

Similarly, Neo from *The Matrix* was always the One but never believed he was the One. Neo's subconscious mind, with limited beliefs, programmed him since childhood and boxed him by his conditioning. Morpheus, through the power of suggestion, gradually but consistently implanted the seed of belief in Neo. Slowly but surely, the implanted seed grew to blossom as experiential, knowing in Neo that he was the One. The empirical knowing that he was the One manifested superpower to defy physical laws and function as the super character The One, instead of being a feeble conditioned reactor in the Matrix. The movie Matrix is not a science fiction movie but rather a documentary about human capacity and human limited conditioning by society.

This is the Truth about every human being, according to the Seers, Sages, and Prophets. We are more than our conditioned mind, body, personal identity, or ego. We are the limitless, formless, shapeless, birthless, deathless, and timeless field of beingness. We are a field of energy that is beyond space and time; we are the creator of the manifested within time and space. The creator of this Universe is no(thing) and no object and cannot be seen or observed by anything. In the same way, a knife cannot cut itself or the eyes can see the world but cannot see themselves.

"To be happy with yourself in the present moment while maintaining a dream of your future is a grand recipe for manifestation. When you feel so whole that you no longer care whether "it" will happen, that's when amazing things materialize before your eyes. I've learned that being whole is the perfect state of creation. I've seen this time and time again in witnessing true healing in people all over the world. They feel so complete that they no longer want, no longer feel lack, and no longer try to do it themselves. They let go, and to their amazement, something greater than they are responding—and they laugh at the simplicity of the process." —

Joe Dispenza, You Are the Placebo.

We are like fish in the middle of the ocean in search of water, lost, hopeless, and confused with too many theistic and atheistic theories without realizing we are in the ocean of love and grace. The personality, ego, and identity can never see the True Self, but it is Self-Aware that it exists. The only way we realize our True Self is by the power of suggestion, and gradually but consistently believing in this Truth until we transcend all our conditioning, limitations, subconscious tendencies, genetics, memory, imagination, body, mind, and so on. As soon as we transcend the Karmic, genetic, subconscious, and lifetime memories and their tendencies, the sooner we break free from the bondage of this limited mind and body. We become the non-mental knowing awareness.

According to *Tell Yourself a Better Lie* by best-selling author Marisa Peer, we are telling ourselves an outdated childhood lie that was based on a narrative and image we had as a child. "Through ten diverse case studies, Marisa explains how our unmet needs as children can morph into fixed stories we tell ourselves in adulthood—and, more importantly, how we all have the power to change them. If you have been longing for a happier, more fulfilled life, pick up *Tell Yourself a Better Lie* and take control of your own story today."

You are living a mind-created lie; you do not think you are better off creating a better story to identify and live as superior beings. All it takes is a shift in perception and really believing in it as we believe in this false mind-created identity. The greatest power that I have realized is our own beliefs and the focus of our attention.

I have decided to choose to identify as my True Universal identity and use this personal identity without any attachment or judgment for daily activity. I know if every human being does the same, then we do not need to be followers, and it will not be a top-down leadership society. Every being will identify as the Universal Self to serve the Universal Self minus personal ego.

Everyone will harmoniously live in peace as One Universal Self, and we will not have one Gandhi, one Martin Luther King, one Jesus Christ, one Muhammad (PBUH), or one Buddha because we realize the Truth in us, that we are One, we are their same One Consciousness. It would be a bottom-up, leaderless society where everyone will have the same cause and identity, where all humans will live for a Universal cause rather than a personal egoistic hoarding limited selfish cause. It is time for humanity to transcend the limited competitive identity and evolve into mature, cooperative people, transforming the earth into the heaven it was originally designed to be for all its inhabitants.

Love stays in the now and appreciates the contentment, joy, and happiness that shine from the presence in the now. Either we deliberately create tools to stay in now, or our subconscious mind will automatically, out of the evolutionary process, habits, and conditionings, create default habitual tools to keep us in the illusion of the now, contentment, and happiness. Then, our subconscious mind habitually creates unhealthy habits like gambling, drinking, drugs, overeating, shopping, sex, and all things that will enhance the senses that keep us in bondage and the illusion of presence away from our busy minds and thoughts.

On the other hand, we can consciously create healthy tools and deliberate habits such as yoga, meditation, exercise, hiking, and nature walks to stay in the present and the now. It does not matter whether we are consciously or unconsciously creating unhealthy or healthy habits; the root cause of happiness and joy is found in being present in the now without our mind and egoistic thoughts intruding on our peace and joy.

The Dynamics of Manifestation

The enhancement of our sensory system pulls our attention to the present, giving us the illusion of temporary contentment. However, we can cultivate a mindful presence from a place of awareness. It is best to deliberately stay present in the now and create tools to bring your focus back to the present moment. Do not become a victim of your habitual mind.

Through evolutionary progress, the body and mind are genetically programmed to promote or impede life activities. This system has developed chemical receptors in the brain that reward or punish us, helping to program our DNA with certain habits and tendencies. This reward and punishment system has evolved over millions of years to improve our chances of survival and reproduction. According to research, this system involves a complex interplay of neurotransmitters and neural circuits, particularly in the limbic system and prefrontal cortex that govern our emotional and motivational responses [21]. The chemicals in charge of this system, which I call the heaven and hell on earth chemicals, include:

- **Glutamate & GABA:** Glutamate acts as the throttle, playing an important role in learning and memory, but too much can lead to agitation, impulsive behavior, and even violence. GABA, the brake, increases tranquility by inhibiting excessive nerve activity. [22]

- **Serotonin:** Serotonin is associated with serenity and hopefulness in moods. SSRIs aim to increase serotonin levels to combat depression. [23]

- **Dopamine:** Dopamine is our arousal and stimulation neurotransmitter, associated with rewards like sex, eating, pleasure, and creative thinking. Both low and high levels can lead to issues like depression or dependence. [24]

- **Endorphins:** These are powerful hormones and neurotransmitters released during stress or pain, reducing pain and inducing euphoria. Foods like chocolate and chili peppers can enhance endorphin secretion. [25]

---

[21] https://www.ncbi.nlm.nih.gov/books/NBK92798/

[22] https://my.clevelandclinic.org/health/articles/22839-glutamate

[23] https://www.healthline.com/health/mental-health/serotonin

[24] https://www.webmd.com/mental-health/what-isdopamine#:~:text=Dopamine%20is%20a%20complex%20hormone,like%20Parkinson's%2 0disease%20and%20schizophrenia.

[25]

https://www.medicinenet.com/endorphins_natural_pain_and_stress_fighters/views.htm#:

~:text=Endorphins%20are%20among%20the%20brain,signals%20within%20the%20

- **Noradrenaline** (norepinephrine): The main neurotransmitter of the sympathetic nervous system, linked to the fight-or-flight response and regulating heart rate and blood pressure. Imbalances can cause sleepiness or nervousness. [26]

This reward and punishment system significantly impacts your psychological and emotional well-being, promoting survivorship, reproduction, and the transmission of our genes. These chemicals define our experiences and perception of reality on earth.

The use of drugs manipulates the production and use of these chemicals, making us dependent. Some pharmaceuticals help curb drug addiction by blocking receptors, but this can lead to depression and suicidal thoughts.

Therefore, it is crucial to let our body and mind organically produce these chemicals without external manipulation, synchronizing our energies with the field of awareness. Being deliberate about our habits and tendencies allows us to promote our reward system for life activities that help us physically, emotionally, mentally, and spiritually, such as deliberately choosing the right things and amounts of eating, drinking, working, sleeping, walking, exercising, and reading.

I used to eat three or even four times a day, driven by psychological rather than physical hunger. Recognizing this, I decided to become aware of my mind rewarding my body every time I ate. I convinced myself that I ate out of habit, not necessity, and substituted food with alkalized water with electrolytes. For the past two years, I've eaten only once a day with my family, except on special occasions. This daily fasting has kept me at a comfortable weight, and I feel good instead of bloated. A small, deliberate shift from bad habits to good habits creates a new paradigm. The newer, always aware you will manifest an even better version of yourself.

My family acknowledges my evolution and changes so profound that, except for my external image, they don't recognize the new me. I don't recognize my old self, which was pretentious, egoistic, misogynistic, and self-centered. Thanks to the power of manifestation, I've reprogrammed

---

nervo us%20system.

[26] https://my.clevelandclinic.org/health/articles/22610-norepinephrinenoradrenaline#:~:text=Norepinephrine%20(Noradrenaline)-,Norepinephrine%20(Noradrenaline),short%2Dterm%20serious%20health%20situatio ns.

my old paradigm with a new transcendent True self.

Through manifestation, I've unprogrammed my subconscious mind to reprogram it with a better paradigm. This transcendence happens at the subconscious level. While self-improvement courses can initially motivate, the subconscious mind often reverts to old habits when it becomes uncomfortable.

Dr. Bruce Lipton states, "the subconscious mind dictates 95% everything we do. It's our subconscious beliefs that dictate our behavior and the results we experience in our lives. We are only conscious of less than 5% of our thoughts throughout any given day."

The programming, reprogramming, unlearning, and relearning must occur at the subconscious level to make a lasting difference. Many people study self-inquiry but don't experience the Truth because they only understand and memorize concepts. True change requires reprogramming the subconscious mind.

The subconscious mind is a concept that has fascinated scientists and philosophers for centuries. It is often likened to the vast, invisible part of an iceberg submerged beneath the water's surface, representing the powerful undercurrent of our psyche. This part of our mind plays a significant role in shaping our behavior, personality, ego, addictions, beliefs, and daily activities. The subconscious mind's evolution can be traced back to the earliest forms of life, where even single-celled organisms exhibited a primitive responsiveness to their environment. This responsiveness is seen as a precursor to consciousness. As life evolved and multicellular organisms developed, the complexity of their nervous systems increased, leading to more sophisticated subconscious processing. Eventually, in higher mammals, a new level of awareness emerged—self-consciousness or the conscious mind.

Despite the conscious mind's ability to think critically and make deliberate choices, the subconscious mind still operates as our "autopilot." It influences approximately 95% of our daily actions through ingrained patterns and learned behaviors. These automatic responses are often based on past experiences, memories, and beliefs stored deep within the subconscious. Because of this, we can sometimes find ourselves acting out of habit, unaware of the underlying programming that drives our behavior. Without conscious effort to understand and reprogram the subconscious mind, we risk becoming slaves to these habitual patterns, like zombies following a script written by our past experiences and conditioning.

To reprogram the subconscious mind and gain greater control over our actions and beliefs, we can:

- Practice repetition and mindfulness: Consistently introducing new, positive beliefs and behaviors through repetition helps replace old patterns. Mindfulness allows us to observe our thoughts and feelings without judgment, making us aware of the subconscious programming that needs change.

- • Energy modalities offer profound pathways to reprogram the subconscious mind and transform our deeply ingrained paradigms by directly addressing the energetic patterns that influence our thoughts and behaviors. Techniques like **PSYCH-K** aim to facilitate rapid belief change by engaging both hemispheres of the brain to rewrite limiting subconscious programs. **Light therapy** utilizes specific wavelengths to affect mood and circadian rhythms, potentially enhancing mental well-being and alleviating depressive symptoms. **Acupuncture**, rooted in ancient Chinese medicine, involves inserting fine needles at specific points to stimulate energy flow along the body's meridians, which may help release blockages and restore harmony between mind and body. **Tapping**, or **Emotional Freedom Techniques (EFT),** combines elements of cognitive therapy and acupressure, allowing individuals to alleviate stress and negative emotions by tapping on specific points while focusing on troubling thoughts. Hypnosis accesses the subconscious in a relaxed state, making it more receptive to positive suggestions and new perspectives. Meditation and visualization practices cultivate mindfulness and intentional thought patterns, promoting inner peace and clarity. While scientific evidence supporting these modalities varies, many people report significant benefits such as reduced anxiety, improved emotional resilience, and the release of limiting beliefs. By embracing these energy modalities, individuals can effectively shed old patterns and install new, empowering ones, accelerating personal growth and transformation.

Understanding the subconscious mind is not just an exploration of our primal instincts but also a reflection of the evolutionary journey of consciousness itself. By becoming aware of and actively engaging with our subconscious, we can transcend automatic behaviors and align more closely with our True Self. This process allows us to live more consciously and purposefully, free from the limitations of past conditioning and open to the infinite possibilities of conscious creation.

From my experience, faith and belief are the foundation manifestation. Your constant attention to your faith and belief frames your manifestation. Slowly, faith and belief become an innate knowing. In the same way, I knew I had the power of a deliberate cocreator in my lucid dreams, manifesting from a place of wholeness, worthiness, and abundance. When you meditate to realize the Truth within, you become whole and one without judgment, wants, needs, desires, or temptations. The personal identity, regardless of its knowledge of manifestation, cannot manifest as easily as the innate intelligence of wholeness, which has no wants, needs, desires, or temptations. So, it is best practice to become one with the frequency of innate intelligence in wholeness or meditation then visualize in appreciation what you want as if you already have.

The best practice for becoming whole, complete, and abundant is to embrace meditation and cultivate a state of emptiness. From this foundation, harmonize all your energies—physical, mental, emotional, spiritual, and environmental—positively. This means nurturing your physical body and mind with healthy food, drink, thoughts, and entertainment, as well as education and feelings that uplift rather than taint your energy.

Your environment plays a critical role in influencing your energy. Both immediate and distant environments affect your state of harmony. To create a truly positive energy field, ensure that everyone in your close circle—family, friends, and loved ones—aligns with your positive and blessed energy. Surround yourself with supportive and uplifting individuals who contribute to this harmony.

If your environment is not conducive to positivity, take steps to change it. Remember, you cannot change others, but you can change yourself and your surroundings. If you find yourself among negative people, distance yourself, even if it means facing temporary loneliness or discomfort. This space from negativity is crucial for maintaining your positive energy and manifesting your desires.

Let go of relationships and situations that limit you, no matter how important they may seem. Holding onto negativity only hinders your progress. Instead, focus on your desires, release them, and remain whole, content, and grateful, as if you already possess everything you seek.

Patience is key. In a society addicted to instant gratification, embracing patience allows you to align with the natural flow of life and create lasting abundance.

Abraham Hicks beautifully explains that if a train is going 100 miles an hour in the wrong direction, it can't instantly change direction and go 100 miles an hour in the right direction. It takes time to slow down, stop, and then gain momentum in the right direction. Have patience, get in the right feeling or vibration, stop, and then move in the right direction.

"The universal law of attraction never yields to you something different from your vibrational frequency. So, when you say, 'Okay, I get it. I can find softer thoughts and every day I'll get better at it,' and as you do, you will turn and go with the current. Immediately, you will start feeling better. And people who are watching you will say, 'What's changed? Did you get that job you were looking for? Or did you get over that illness? Or did the money that you needed come in?' And you will say, 'No.' 'Then why are you so happy?' 'I know it is illogical,' you will say. Because what I thought I needed to be happy hasn't happened yet. I've just stopped doing what was making me unhappy. And I felt better.' And then say to them, 'And I think I am on the right track. I don't think you can feel this good without good things beginning to flow into your experience.' Those would be the most accurate words that you could ever speak. You can't feel negative emotions and let the good stuff in, and you can't feel positive emotions and keep the good stuff out. You just can't." —

Abraham Hicks.

From a broken place when I started my journey to finding my True Self, I have manifested absolute clarity in seeing the Truth without my eyes, knowing the Truth without my mind, and being the Truth without my body. I started this awakening journey broken, lost, empty, hopeless, and extremely pretentious. I reached contentment and wholeness without fame, money, or materialistic things. There is nothing wrong with materialistic things, money, and fame, especially money, because money is neutral. It can take any shape or color like water. Money itself is neutral until you use it for the good of your loved ones and others or not.

Money is not evil; what we do with it determines its value. Materialistic things bring comfort but not happiness, joy, or contentment, which come from within. I practiced manifestation for clarity of knowing the Truth, realizing that clarity is the path to joy and contentment without fame and riches.

Most people want to manifest money, fame, love, joy, and contentment in that order. I found unconditional contentment from within by realizing my True Self. Like a flower doesn't need external perfume because its aroma is its essence, realize the flower in you and sweeten your experience and surroundings with your essence.

I promised to share an example of my awareness of witnessing the drama of everyday life, so here we go. I wake up, my brain becomes active, and perception begins as I open my eyes. Thoughts flood my perception, but I remain aware of them, pulling my attention back to me and thanking the universe for giving me breath, my senses, my family, health, and the true knowing of the Truth.

I go to work appreciating my workers, neighbors, customers, and life in general. Every day is a new vibrational point of attraction, allowing me to create a new reality. Customers come in upset about problems with their products or services, but I embrace them with empathy instead of defensiveness. I ask about their day and if they feel blessed and their protective walls go down.

My wife calls me upset with a problem, and I listen, supporting her. The old me might have judged and defended myself, but the new me is empathic and whole. Our relationship has improved, though some old habits persist, and I remain aware of them.

Thoughts of work, customers, and home flood my brain, but I remain aware of them. I meditate, my habitual mind floods with thoughts, and I acknowledge them. Thoughts of unnecessary eating or watching a movie come up, but I witness them. This practice allows me to watch life from my True Self instead of getting caught up in it.

One day, I was at home and fell asleep in the living room, planning to rest for half an hour before bed. My habitual mind kept talking about my day's experiences, but I remained aware of it. In this state, I was halfway between dreaming and waking, aware of both.

As the ego self-fell asleep, my inner voice narrated the ego's state. I watched the ego and habitual mind resist sleep, eventually winning the battle to remain awake. I had an epiphany: my True Self, the true witness, is separate from my habitual mind and ego.

I woke up, opened my eyes, and became aware of my surroundings and habitual thoughts. I experienced True awareness understanding that thoughts, emotions, perceptions, experiences, and the ego are within but perceived to be separate from the real Self.

During my nightly reflections, I recognize that all external occurrences of the day, perceived through my senses, thoughts, and emotions, transpire within the realm of a singular, all-encompassing Awareness, transcending the notions of "self" and "ownership". The True Self goes beyond "I am", "Self", and "ownership", being everything (because it is whole, all-encompassing without ownership), nothing (because nothing in my experience can be compared to it and it is not a thing), and everywhere (because it is infinite and has no end). This reflection is the key understanding of my book, but your ego will overlook it.

Rene Descartes said, "I think, therefore I am," but I believe, "I am Aware, therefore I am." Thoughts and everything in your perception of experiences are transient and secondary to the real constant Self, which is Awareness.

Understanding how the mind and its focus can profoundly impact on our experiences is essential. The parable of The Farmer and the Seed illustrates this concept perfectly. Just as the farmer's shift in focus transformed his barren fields into a bountiful harvest, our awareness and intentional focus can shape our realities and influence our experiences in profound ways.

"There once was a farmer who struggled year after year with his crops. The land was fertile, and his neighbors produced an abundance of fruits and vegetables. Yet, the farmer's harvest remained meager.

One day, a wise old woman from a nearby village noticed the farmer's despair. She approached him and asked, "Why do your crops yield so little when the land is so rich?"

The farmer sighed and explained, "I've tried everything. I work hard to plant the best seeds, but my harvest always disappoints."

The woman smiled and said, "Perhaps the problem isn't the seeds or your work but your focus."

Intrigued, the farmer asked, "What do you mean?"

The woman explained, "You focus on the lack in your fields, the meagerness of your harvest. Your thoughts and worries create a vibration of scarcity. Instead, try focusing on abundance. Imagine your fields overflowing with plump vegetables and juicy fruits. Feel the joy of a successful harvest."

The farmer was skeptical, but he decided to give it a try. The next season, he planted his seeds with a new mindset. He visualized bountiful crops, felt the satisfaction of a full harvest, and expressed gratitude for the land's potential.

As the season progressed, the farmer noticed a change. His crops grew stronger and healthier than ever before. He tended to them with renewed hope, and come harvest time; his fields were indeed overflowing with abundance.

The farmer finally understood the woman's words. His focus on lack had manifested scarcity, while his shift towards abundance had yielded a plentiful harvest."

Just as the farmer's transformation from focusing on scarcity to embracing abundance led to a bountiful harvest, we, too, have the power to influence our lives through our thoughts and perceptions. By shifting our attention from the limitations and challenges we face to the possibilities and opportunities available to us, we align ourselves with a more positive and productive energy. This alignment enables us to harness our inner potential and create the changes we desire. As we cultivate our fields of existence with mindfulness and deliberate intention, we open ourselves up to a more fulfilling and enriched experience. Embracing this lesson empowers us to transcend our habitual patterns and engage in the creative process of manifesting our desired reality. Just as the farmer's fields flourished with a renewed focus, so too can our lives flourish when we consciously direct our energy toward the abundance that lies within and around us. Remember, true power lies not in what we have but in our ability to perceive and create the reality we wish to live in.

Chapter 9

The Layers of Existence

"In our quest to understand reality, we must expand our perception beyond the limits of what we see."—

Albert Einstein

Our universe is perceived to exist within three dimensions of space: up and down, forward and backward, left and right. The fourth dimension, as commonly understood, is time. However, this is only our limited perception of reality. Humanity has yet to evolve enough to recognize the existence of numerous other dimensions that remain imperceptible to us.

As I have argued earlier, time is largely an illusion—except for the present moment. Let us assume, for the sake of discussion that time exists but is inherently relative. It is relative to your consciousness and perception. For instance, when you're thoroughly enjoying yourself, time seems to disappear, and hours can pass in what feels like mere moments. The more you remain present in the now, the less significant time becomes.

Time is not a constant; it varies relative to perception, gravity, and mass. Under stronger gravitational forces, time slows down—a phenomenon supported by Einstein's theory of relativity. Similarly, time is tied to mass. If particles had no mass, time would lose its relevance entirely.

This relativity highlights how the limits of our perception shape our understanding of time and dimensions. As we expand our awareness and consciousness, we may uncover the hidden dimensions that influence the fabric of existence, redefining our understanding of reality.

Consider the GPS as an example. It was originally designed and owned by the US military, and the generals/military personnel in charge of the project were undereducated in science. They should have taken the relativity of time into account, and the GPS initially did not work properly. Scientists had to explain to the generals that time is relative to the gravitational force: the closer you are to the earth's surface, the slower time becomes; further away from the earth's surface, the faster time goes. Although the earth's gravity is weak and the time difference is unnoticeable, it is still measurable [27]. This fact allows us to deduce that time should slow down to nothing and cannot exist at the center of a black hole, where the gravitational force is immensely great. According to Einstein's theory of gravity, time does not exist at the center of a black hole .[28]

Three dimensions of space and one dimension of time are needed for the body and mind to experience this reality. This is how we experience and perceive our universe and reality. It's okay for the mind and body to function in this reality if we do not identify with its experiences or functions. It is crucial to be self-aware and remind yourself that you are aware of this body and mind experiencing reality in these dimensions.

Imagine watching a 3D movie where the director masterfully draws you into the story, engaging you emotionally, mentally, and even physically, especially in thrilling scenes. This immersive experience mirrors how the Universe and God have designed your senses to be deeply involved in the illusions of this world. These illusions can be so captivating that they obscure the clear reality and your true self. Your ultimate purpose is to realize this Truth and align your identity with it.

Now, picture reality as a movie playing on a 3D screen, with you watching the movie. Becoming mentally, emotionally, and completely attached to the 3D movie, as if you are part of it. However, even when you are deeply involved, you do not identify with the movie or its characters. You can detach from the movie emotionally and mentally simply by shifting your attention away from it knowing that it is just a movie, and you are the detached observer. Similarly, you can watch the play of life on the screen of One Awareness as a detached observer.

The purpose of this illusion is to provide a dynamic and immersive environment for growth and self-realization. By navigating through these illusions, you gain experiences and insights that ultimately lead you to recognize and align with the deeper Truth of your existence. This journey through illusions helps you to understand your true nature and purpose,

---

[27] https://www.nasa.gov/image-article/einsteins-theory-of-relativity-critical-gps-seendistant-stars/
[28] https://www.space.com/17661-theory-general-relativity.html

fostering spiritual growth and enlightenment. Our sensory system evolved to experience this world as the reality we perceive, but that does not mean our perception of the world and universe is true. Our perception of this world's reality is designed to promote the survival of the fittest, reproduction, and experiencing of thriving and contrasting life forms on earth, but it does not constitute the actual truth.

Donald D. Hoffman, a professor of cognitive science at the University of California, Irvine, has spent the past three decades studying perception, artificial intelligence, evolutionary game theory, and the brain. His conclusion is dramatic: the world presented to us by our perceptions is nothing like reality. He says we have evolution itself to thank for this magnificent illusion, as it maximizes evolutionary fitness by driving truth to extinction.

"The classic argument is that those of our ancestors who saw more accurately had a competitive advantage over those who saw less accurately and thus were more likely to pass on their genes that coded for those more accurate perceptions, so after thousands of generations, we can be quite confident that we're the offspring of those who saw accurately, and so we see accurately. That sounds very plausible. But I think it is utterly false. It misunderstands the fundamental fact about evolution, which is that it is about fitness functions — mathematical functions that describe how well a given strategy achieves the goals of survival and reproduction.

This perspective is supported by various scientific studies and research in the fields of cognitive science and evolutionary biology. For instance, the theory of "perceptual bias" suggests that our senses are tuned to pick up certain types of information more than others, leading to a biased view of reality that favors survival and reproduction rather than accuracy.[29]

Research by neuroscientists like V.S. Ramachandran has shown how our brain constructs perceptions based on limited sensory input, often filling in gaps and creating coherent experiences that may not reflect objective reality. In his work on visual perception, Ramachandran has demonstrated how the brain uses shortcuts, known as heuristics, to

---

[29]

https://catalogofbias.org/biases/perceptionbias/#:~:text=Perception%20bias%20is%20the%20tendency,influenced%20by%20percepti on%20biases%20unconsciously.

interpret sensory data quickly, often at the expense of accuracy .[30]

Studies in evolutionary psychology have explored how evolutionary pressures shape our cognitive processes. Leda Cosmides and John Tooby have argued that the human mind consists of specialized modules that evolved to solve specific problems faced by our ancestors. These modules are optimized for survival and reproduction, not for discovering the ultimate truth about the universe .[31]

The mathematical physicist Chetan Prakash proved a theorem that I devised that says: According to evolution by natural selection, an organism that sees reality as it is will never be more fit than an organism of equal complexity that sees none of reality but is just tuned to fitness." –

Donald Hoffman.

Research has shown that what we see is not a direct representation of the world but rather a constructed image created by our brains. The perception of concepts and experiences of our reality is what is constructed by the lens of our mind, which is primarily affected by our conditioning, beliefs, genetic programming, and both conscious and subconscious mind. The phenomenon of "change blindness [32]," for example, illustrates how we can fail to notice significant changes in our visual field when our attention is focused elsewhere, highlighting the limitations and selective nature of our perception.

The Reticular Activating System (RAS)

The Reticular Activating System (RAS) is a fascinating phenomenon that showcases how our brains are wired to prioritize survival and reproduction, often at the expense of perceiving the complete truth. Known colloquially as the "red Ferrari syndrome," the RAS demonstrates how our attention is programmed to focus on what is deemed most important for our immediate survival and reproductive success. Located in the brainstem, the RAS is a network of neurons that plays a crucial role

---

30

https://www.researchgate.net/publication/233556531_The_Science_of_Art_A_Neur ologica l_Theory_of_Aesthetic_Experience

[31] http://cogweb.ucla.edu/ep/EP-primer.html

[32] https://www.healthline.com/health/what-is-change-blindness-and-why-does-it-happen

in regulating arousal and consciousness. It acts as a filter, deciding which incoming stimuli are significant enough to enter our conscious awareness and which can be disregarded. This selective focus is essential for functioning in a complex and often dangerous world.

The RAS evolved as an adaptive mechanism to help early humans remain alert to potential dangers and opportunities, such as predators, food sources, and potential mates. By filtering out irrelevant information and honing in on critical stimuli, the RAS enabled our ancestors to react swiftly and efficiently to their environment. This focus on survival and reproduction often means overlooking broader truths or more nuanced aspects of reality that are not immediately relevant to these goals. For example, in a modern context, once someone decides to buy a red Ferrari, they suddenly start noticing red Ferraris everywhere. This happens because the RAS is tuned to filter out other vehicles and highlight what it considers important based on recent thoughts or desires, reflecting its deep-seated evolutionary programming.

Key Benefits of the RAS:

- The RAS helps us concentrate on specific tasks by filtering out unnecessary or distracting information, allowing us to maintain focus and achieve our goals.

- It plays a critical role in regulating transitions between sleep and wakefulness, ensuring that we are alert and responsive when necessary.

- By prioritizing certain stimuli, especially those related to threats or opportunities, the RAS enhances our survival instincts and ensures that we remain vigilant in potentially dangerous situations.

- As one of the oldest parts of the brain, the RAS has been preserved and refined throughout human evolution due to its significant benefits in awareness and responsiveness. It was advantageous for early humans to focus on immediate survival and reproduction, filtering out less critical information to concentrate on what mattered most for their survival in an unpredictable environment.

Understanding the role of the RAS provides insight into how our brains filter reality, focusing on what is essential for survival and reproduction while often neglecting other aspects of the truth. This filtering process, while beneficial in many ways, can limit our perception, causing us to overlook broader perspectives or deeper truths beyond our immediate concerns.

Here's a simple, yet effective, morning meditation routine to help you focus on attracting abundance of happiness, health, and wealth into your life:

Morning Meditation for Abundance

Prepare Your Space:

Find a quiet and comfortable place to sit or lie down. Set the intention to focus on your goals for happiness, health, love, and wealth.

Relax and Breathe:

Close your eyes and take a few deep breaths, inhaling through your nose for three seconds, hold it for three seconds, and exhaling through your mouth for six seconds. Focus on your breath, allowing yourself to become fully present in the moment. Let the feelings, emotions, and thoughts come and go on the screen of your Awareness. You are aware of your feelings, emotions, and thoughts but nothing is aware of you. So, remain in this detached empty Awareness watch the transients come and go out of your reality.

Affirmations for Abundance:

Silently or aloud, repeat affirmations that resonate with you.

Some examples include:

"I am grateful for the happiness, health, love, and wealth in my life."

"I attract positive energy and abundance."

"I am worthy of happiness, health, love, and wealth."

Write down your own affirmations for manifestation.

Visualize Your Goals:

Imagine a bright light at the base of your skull, representing your RAS. Visualize this light expanding and filtering through your mind, helping you focus on your goals.

Picture yourself achieving your desires: seeing yourself happy, healthy, in love, and wealthy.

Feel the Emotions:

Connect with the emotions of having already achieved your goals and affirmations. Do not just say your affirmations but show gratitude as if you already have them in your experience, use your imagination.

Feel the joy, contentment, and peace that come with having an abundance of happiness, health, love, and wealth. Be aware of your subconscious mind and the tendencies that limit you. Develop the habit of identifying and disregarding limiting beliefs, habits, and tendencies.

Anchor Your Intentions:

As you continue to breathe deeply, mentally anchor your intentions for the day.

Repeat to yourself:

"I am focused, I am capable, and I am manifesting abundance in my life."

Conclude Your Meditation:

Slowly bring your awareness back to the present moment.

Open your eyes, stretch your body, and carry positive energy with you throughout the day.

Tips for Consistency:

Try to meditate at the same time every morning as soon as you wake up from deep sleep to build a routine. Keep a journal to note down any thoughts, feelings, or insights that come up during your meditation.

This practice can help tune your RAS to prioritize and manifest the abundance you seek. Remember, consistency and earnestness are key in making this a powerful habit that will align your focus and energy with your goals. Enjoy your journey towards a more abundant and fulfilling life!

My truth is that I am using my body and mind in the realm of this illusion of worldly reality, which took millions of years of evolution to produce the instrument of my sensation. This sensation is witnessed by not a thing but a universal supreme innate intelligence that is present everywhere, independent of time and space. My body, mind, ego, and personal identity are inside my consciousness, and my consciousness, which is the union of my physical and metaphysical self, is within awareness.

Everything from a particle of an atom to rocks, grass, and the essence of every living being is the presence of this fundamental field of awareness. This awareness has no contrast and is the same one in all beings before the consciousness and the form. After surgery, you wake up and say, "I was unconscious." Who was aware of

unconsciousness? It is the witness of the sense of "I am" before you veil it with a false identity. This creator is all the creation, which is everything and nothing (the shapeless, formless, limitless, boundless, and timeless) in the fundamental field of awareness as and in oneness.

At the end of this chapter, I will narrate from the awareness point of view, watching the movie of my body and mind in action. It is more evident when we study our behavior as a species, like studying other species sharing this earth with us. Suppose we detach ourselves and study our behavioral patterns, like studying lab rats in a conditioned space. In that case, it becomes evident how we, much like these lab rats, become accustomed to our comfort zones and conditioned mindsets. Try to see your daily routine and the way you act and react throughout the day from a detached perspective, like you are studying a subject other than yourself. You will see how most of your actions were unnecessary and impulsive. Most of the things you say and do throughout the day are not even necessary because not everything requires a reaction; sometimes, you have to do is be present and observe as the witness to your reality.

Our conscious and subconscious minds communicate in a bidirectional way. One command and the other follows. Our actions are almost always driven by our subconscious, where heaps of signals are generated and sent to the conscious mind. However, the conscious mind is logical and analytical. Out of 11 million bits of information per second produced by our five senses, only 40 bits are used by our conscious minds for thinking, planning, decision-making, etc.

The subconscious mind is vast and imaginative, with no boundaries, while the conscious mind is logical and analytical, as it has to deal with reality and react according to the stimuli around us. The subconscious isn't logical and analytical like the conscious mind; it doesn't distinguish between fantasy and reality. It uses the language of symbols, pictures, and metaphors to communicate ideas to your conscious mind.

These two levels of your mind work together to determine your actions. They can bring you failure or success, anxiety or happiness, and frustration or achievements. It all comes down to how you use them. You cannot outdo your image of yourself that is stored in the subconscious mind, and this is the main cause of what prevents us from achieving our goals. Have you ever not asked someone on a date or not applied for a job because you feared failure? This is the subconscious mind at work. If we do not have an image of our success in the unconscious mind, achieving consistent success is practically impossible.

The conscious and subconscious minds are carefully wired together. Old connections are continually breaking, and new ones are forming.

One of the things that determine how these connections form is your thoughts. You can use your conscious mind to shape your unconscious mind by overriding it. This is a challenging process. It requires consistency. But it can be done through active awareness and being in the now.

An average human mind generates around 70,000 to 100,000 thoughts per day. Now, do you think all of these are conscious? If you were aware of all these thoughts every day, you might go insane from data overload. That's why half of it is happening on the backend, without us even realizing it, because not all thoughts are some "statements" exactly. They can be a subconscious signal, controlling how we feel about ourselves and the world around us.

Once we self-automate our thought patterns to be in the now, positive thoughts come just as naturally as negative ones, and this leads to making better, clearer decisions without feeling drained or decision-fatigued. Yes, decision fatigue is actually a thing. You may think it's not a big deal to choose what to wear or what to eat each morning as you start your day, but doing that over and over gets tiring for the mind without us knowing. Even trivial things like driving to work or checking social media can take up thousands of decision energy units. According to researchers, an average person makes about 180 decisions per minute, even for a small task like driving. Imagine how many you're making right now, just sitting there reading this book.

Often, our thoughts occur so quickly that we fail to notice them, but they can still affect our mood indirectly. Having negative automatic thoughts is somehow more common, though; it just comes naturally to us. To break your pattern and reshape it, you need to start by identifying these negative thoughts. Then, we can eventually replace them with new rational thoughts by directing our focus to the now and staying aware.

The Philosophy of Spinoza

Spinoza was born in 1632 in Amsterdam to a prominent family of moderate means in Amsterdam's Portuguese-Jewish community. As a boy, he was one of the star pupils in the congregation's Talmud Torah school and was likely being groomed for a career as a rabbi. However, at the age of seventeen, he was forced to cut short his formal studies to help run the family's importing business.

On July 27, 1656, Spinoza was issued the harshest writ of herem (ban or ex-communication) ever pronounced by the Sephardic community of Amsterdam; it was never rescinded. While the exact reasons for his excommunication remain unknown, it is believed that Spinoza's ideas, which later appeared in his philosophical treatises, were the cause. In these works, Spinoza denies the immortality of the soul, rejects the notion of a transcendent, providential God, and claims that the Law (the commandments of the Torah and rabbinic legal principles) was neither literally given by God nor any longer binding on Jews .[33]

Despite these radical views, Spinoza did not declare himself an atheist. He insisted that he remained a faithful defender of God, albeit with a different conception of God than traditionally accepted.

"Whatever is, is in God, and nothing can exist or be conceived without God." —

Spinoza.

Spinoza denied the idea of personal immortality and the notion of rewards or punishments after death. He believed that such ideas give rise to superstition, enslaving the mind to imagination and distracting us from the present. According to Spinoza, any rewards for our virtues are in this life. He held that a life spent in imagination is one without reason, lived in servitude rather than gratitude.

---

[33] https://plato.stanford.edu/entries/spinoza/#Biog

Spinoza believed that when we die, we cease to exist, as there is no personal immortality or life after death. Most people identify with their body, mind, ego, earthly accomplishments, and false identity, so when this false image ceases to exist, we cease to exist. He argued that it is better to realize our true awareness before the death of our impermanent false self.

This concept aligns with the Sufi teaching, "To die before you die," which emphasizes transcending the false self to discover the true self.

"To become spiritual, you must die to self and come alive in the Lord. Only then will the mysteries of God fall from your lips. To die to self through self-discipline causes suffering but brings you everlasting life." —

Rumi.

Spinoza is transcended from belief to knowing that everything we gain on earth, whether physical, emotional, mental, or identity, must return to earth. Only the true self, the immortal, permanent, and unchanging— Awareness remains.

Spinoza's fundamental principle is the necessary and absolute infinity of God, defined as an infinite being. This concept is the starting point of his philosophy, which is God-centered. In his work "Ethics," Spinoza presents the proof of God's reality through the necessity of a First Cause, a self-caused being [34]. Spinoza believed that God is the sum of the natural and physical laws of the universe, not an individual entity or creator. He argued that God is the substance of the universe, possessing an infinite number of attributes, and thus, all other substances and their attributes in the universe are part of God. Therefore, everything in the universe, from the smallest particle to the largest galaxies, is part of God, and there is nothing in our experience that we could compare God to, so it is Nothing or nothingness from which everything rises and falls, including the idea of you and me.

Spinoza's philosophy on God is that God is not the creator of the world; the world is part of God [35]. This view, often identified as pantheism, conflicts with both Muslim, Jewish, and Christian teachings. For Spinoza, philosophy is a practical endeavor aimed at achieving

---

[34] https://open.bu.edu/handle/2144/9201
[35] https://www.prospectmagazine.co.uk/culture/37996/spinozas-god-einstein-believed-in-it-but-what-was-it

happiness and liberation through an expansion of the mind towards an intuitive understanding of God, nature, and its laws. This understanding leads to "blessedness" or "salvation," which can only be attained by practicing mindfulness and staying in the contemplation and present moment.

Spinoza's God can be seen as the energy we give out to the Universe, highlighting our power to create our reality. Like in the parable "Shelly's Leap of Faith," this transition requires us to step beyond our familiar boundaries and embrace a broader understanding of existence. By doing so, we move from belief to faith and finally to an experiential knowing that liberates us from old constraints and false truths. This shift is essential for true self-awareness and understanding.

"In a tide pool, nestled amongst vibrant coral and swaying seaweed, lived a tiny shrimp named Shelly. Shelly knew her world

well - the smooth pebbles to hide beneath, the gentle current that carried morsels of food, and the looming shadows of larger creatures that sent her darting back into hiding.

One day, a wise hermit crab named Bernard noticed Shelly flitting about. "Shelly," he rumbled, his voice echoing in his borrowed shell,

"Do you ever wonder what lies beyond the tide pool?"

Shelly blinked her beady eyes. "Beyond? There's nothing but the crashing waves and the endless blue."

Bernard chuckled, a soft rasping sound. "Little one, the world stretches far vaster than you can imagine. Coral reefs are teeming with life, sandy beaches where turtles lay their eggs, and the open ocean where whales sing their mournful songs."

Shelly scoffed. "That's impossible! Our world ends at the edge of the pool. How could there be more?"

Bernard smiled patiently. "Imagine, Shelly, that you can only see in two dimensions. You see the flat surface of the water, the length and width of the pool, but not the depth. The world beyond the waves is like a third dimension, unseen by your tiny eyes."

Shelly pondered this. She'd never considered a world beyond the familiar. Yet, sometimes, when the tide receded, she'd glimpse strange, shadowy shapes flitting past the edge of the pool. Could those be the creatures Bernard spoke of?

Driven by curiosity, Shelly decided to venture further than ever before. She clung to a piece of seaweed as it bobbed towards the crashing waves. Fear threatened to engulf her, but the promise of a new world spurred her on.

Suddenly, a giant wave surged, lifting Shelly high above the pool.

Terror gripped her as she tumbled through the air. But then, the wave crested, and for a breathtaking moment, Shelly saw it.

A kaleidoscope of colors stretched before her - vibrant coral gardens, shimmering fish, and a sleek, enormous creature gliding silently through the water. It was a world unlike anything she'd ever imagined, a world that existed beyond the limitations of her tiny world.

Just then, the wave crashed back down, depositing Shelly back into the familiar tide pool. Exhausted but exhilarated, she clung to a rock, forever changed by her glimpse into the unknown.

From that day on, Shelly never saw the pool the same way. She knew her world was part of something much grander, a universe with unseen dimensions waiting to be explored. And though she remained a tiny shrimp, her heart was filled with the wonder of a reality far beyond her limited perception."

Like Shelly, we must be willing to take risks and embrace the unknown to discover the true extent of our potential and the vastness of existence. In doing so, we align with Spinoza's vision of God as the infinite substance of the universe, realizing that our reality is far greater than what we can perceive with our limited senses. As we expand our awareness, we tap into the boundless flow of the universe. This allows our deepest desires to unfold naturally, leading us to a life of harmony with our true nature.

Chapter 10

Cosmic Order and Metaphysical Truths

"All the intricate webs of life are connected; there is nothing truly separate in the universe."—

Unknown

Everything, including the universe and life as we know it, began with the Big Bang. The question of what existed before this monumental event remains one of the greatest mysteries, surrounded by various hypotheses and assumptions. However, the essence of the Big Bang theory is simple: approximately over 13 billion years ago, all current and past matters in the universe came into existence simultaneously. At this pivotal moment, everything was compacted into a singular point of infinite density and unimaginable heat, known as a Singularity. Then, in an event that defies complete human understanding, the Singularity began to expand, giving birth to the universe as we perceive it today.

This expansion wasn't just a physical occurrence but a profound metaphysical event. Before the Big Bang, there was nothing — no time, no matter, no space, and no physical or quantum realities. What existed was an infinite, absolute, formless, timeless, selfless, boundless, and unchanging awareness — a field of nothingness that defies description and is beyond all characteristics. This very field, this "Nothingness," gave rise to the Big Bang and, consequently, to the universe. This ultimate and unchanging awareness is the very essence of everything, the fundamental origin from which our universe was born.

In the first moments after the Big Bang, within the infinitesimally small fraction of a second — 10 to the power of -43rd seconds — the universe was in a state of Oneness, a Singularity where all things were united. As the universe exploded into an inflationary expansion, this oneness began to diversify and spread out. Yet, despite the physical separation, everything remained metaphysically entangled with the fundamental field of awareness, intelligent energy, or Universal Awareness. Since everything began as One, this entanglement remains, connecting all aspects of the universe in a profound, unseen way.

Quantum Entanglement and Universal Oneness

"Quantum entanglement — or 'spooky action at a distance,' as Albert Einstein famously called it, is when two small subatomic particles link together in a certain way when divided no matter at what distance apart, their state remains the same at the quantum physical level. Quantum entanglement is a bizarre, counterintuitive phenomenon that explains how two subatomic particles can be intimately linked to each other even if separated by billions of light-years of space. Despite their vast separation, a change induced in one will affect the other."

If subatomic particles can link together and entangle with one another in an invisible field, then it stands to reason that all matter, dark matter, and dark energy in the universe can be similarly entangled and connected by the invisible and timeless field of Awareness. This connection implies that no matter how vast or divided the universe may become as it continues to expand, everything within it remains One in Oneness, entangled as a whole within the metaphysical field of Awareness.

The interconnectedness of existence is both profound and poetic, encompassing complex concepts that span biology, philosophy, and spirituality.

Biologically, our bodies are ecosystems teeming with trillions of microorganisms, such as the human gut microbiome, which plays a significant role in digestion, immunity, and even mood regulation. While these microorganisms are not conscious in the human sense, they engage in complex interactions essential to our health and survival. Each microorganism, functioning as a tiny part of a larger whole, mirrors the way individual humans participate in the vast web of life on Earth and in the universe. Just as a single bacterium in the body cannot comprehend the identity or purpose of the human being it inhabits; a single person may struggle to grasp the full scope of the global or universal purpose.

Philosophically, the question of individuality and consciousness among microorganisms challenges our understanding of life. Though these organisms do not possess consciousness as we do, their behaviors contribute to the emergent properties of the systems they inhabit, raising questions about the nature of consciousness. Is consciousness a fundamental aspect of the universe, present in all forms of life, or is it an emergent phenomenon that arises from complexity? This debate mirrors the larger existential inquiries humans face when contemplating our place in the universe and the purpose of our existence.

Spiritually, many traditions speak of a universal consciousness that connects all forms of life, suggesting that each being is an expression of a larger, unified reality. This perspective fosters a sense of reverence for life and calls for compassionate action toward all beings, recognizing the interconnectedness of everything. Just as a bacterium is a small part of a vast human ecosystem it cannot fully comprehend, so too is humanity part of a grander cosmic design, often beyond our understanding.

The analogy of a bacterium unable to grasp human existence highlights our own challenge in understanding the universe's vastness and complexity. It serves as a humbling reminder of our place within the cosmos and the limits of our perception.

This journey of our universe, which began from a state of shapeless, formless, timeless, and unchanging Nothingness, is destined to conclude back in that same fundamental invisible field of permanent and constant Nothingness. Herein lies the profound understanding of universal connectedness: the realization that everything is not merely a collection of separate entities but rather expressions of a singular, interconnected whole.

The Role of Consciousness in Universal Awareness

"Consciousness is the eternal witness of the transient." —

Swami Sivananda

Consciousness, as we experience it, is merely a function of Awareness — the union of body, mind, and spirit as a cohesive whole. Yet, while consciousness is fluid, fluctuating between wakefulness, sleep, and unconsciousness, Awareness itself remains constant, unchanging, and absolute. Awareness has no quality, no identity; it is completely shapeless, formless, infinite, and timeless. It is the detached observer, witnessing the comings and goings of consciousness without becoming entangled in its transient manifestations.

Consciousness vs. Awareness:

- **Consciousness:** Subject to change, dependent and influenced by the body, mind, and environment. Consciousness is the subject of transient objects (body, mind, ego, thoughts, imagination, emotions, memory, and so on).

- **Awareness:** Constant, unchanging, and absolute; the detached observer of consciousness and transient objects. Is aware of the subject and objects of our reality.

The experience of consciousness is not absolute because it is subject to change. For instance, we can observe consciousness fading in and out during states of wakefulness and deep sleep. When a person faints, consciousness slowly dissipates until it is entirely lost. Consciousness, as a function of Awareness, thrives on identity, ownership, attachment, shape, purpose, form, quality, personality, experience, and perception. It is in these manifestations that consciousness becomes entangled with the physical world, often leading us to confuse consciousness with Awareness. However, these two are not the same, and conflating them distances us from the Truth.

Awareness, in its true essence, is absolute, constant, unchanging, formless, shapeless, timeless, and a detached witness to all that transpires. To realize this Truth, one must peel back the layers of consciousness, unveiling a subtle, effortless nothingness that transcends the impermanent manifestations of body and mind. Through consistent practice, this transcendence becomes as natural as a game. Even as the body and mind generate countless desires, needs, temptations, fears, worries, sensations, feelings, emotions, perceptions, and experiences, the constant Awareness remains the detached witness, observing these fleeting phenomena as they come and go from one's reality.

"Awareness is the backdrop of all experience, unperturbed by the dramas of life." —

Eckhart Tolle

This constant, unchanging, absolute Awareness is the ultimate Truth the same true essence that permeates everything, both visible and invisible, in the universe. It is this absolute Awareness that realizes a detached seeing, a non-physical seeing, of its manifestations: consciousness, the sense of "I am," experiences, perceptions, and personalities, all of which emerge from a place of nothingness and fall back into nothingness. This is not just my experience but every being's experience of reality but ignored or veiled by mind's evolutionary phenomenon in favor of survival and reproduction.

My daily observations in Oakland reflect a profound understanding of the human condition and the diversity of experiences that shape our communities. It's a powerful reminder of the interconnectedness of all beings and the various paths that life can take.

As I meander through the streets of Oakland, California, near my business with my faithful canine companion, the rich tapestry of humanity unfolds before me. This neighborhood, a vibrant mosaic of cultures and socioeconomic backgrounds, reveals the stark contrasts of life. From the multi-ethnic prostitutes walking in the middle of the street, dressed only in thongs and bras, seeking to survive on the fringes and watched by the shadowy interiors of parked cars, to the bustling activity around Franklin Elementary School, where children are ushered in by parents in vehicles that span the spectrum of wealth. Nearby, the William Chapel Baptist Church becomes a beacon of hope, offering sustenance to a queue of elders from all walks of life. Further along, at Clinton Park, the sun casts its indifferent light on the homeless, whose weary forms adorn park benches—a poignant tableau of despair and addiction. Yet, amidst this diversity, I witness resilience and tradition in the elderly Asian residents, who navigate their way to local markets, their lives interwoven with those of the younger generations they guide.

In every face, regardless of the superficial divisions of race, ethnicity, age, gender, or social standing, I see a shared essence. With each step, I silently offer a benediction for their ultimate happiness and fulfillment, recognizing in them the reflection of a universal consciousness—whether it is called Christ, Buddha, or Mohammad. This consciousness, though often obscured by the layers of physical existence and societal constructs, remains ever-present, connecting us all in the profound unity of being.

These quiet moments of reflection remind me that beneath our visible disparities lies a deeper truth, one that binds us in our shared human experience. Despite our outward differences, we are all threads in the same divine tapestry of existence, each contributing to the rich, intricate fabric of life. In this understanding, I feel a profound connection to every soul I encounter, a connection that transcends the external and reveals the essence of oneness.

Everything attached to the body, mind, identity, and personality is a manifestation of "I am," yet "I am" is seen by consciousness. As the Seer of both consciousness and "I am," you also embody Awareness itself—the Awareness of all the functions of both consciousness and "I am-ness."

In this Awareness, you remain the witness of the body, mind, consciousness, personality, experiences, perceptions, and all that plays out on the screen of Awareness. This understanding highlights the impermanence of all that is born, for anything with a beginning must also have an end.

Only the unchanging, constant Truth endures—birthless, deathless, timeless, and formless. It is in this realization of nothingness and timelessness that the true nature of existence reveals itself, unbound by the cycles of creation and dissolution.

Finding the Truth within yourself — the changeless, birthless, and absolute essence — will free you from the fear of death and the inevitable changes of the body and mind. This Truth, although so obvious and intuitively known on a deeper level, is often resisted by the mind, which fights against it with lies, deceptions, fears, worries, and negative emotions.

For a long time, my own ego fought this realization, attempting to scare my personal identity with thoughts of vanishing from reality. Questions and chatter plagued my mind: *What is this spirituality? Have I ever experienced spirits, ghosts, and mysticism? No, they all must be a bunch of rubbish and nonsense for ignorant illiterates from third-world countries! How can I die before I die? Why can't they articulate everything transparently instead of talking in mysticism? Why can't modern science prove this spirituality to be true? What would happen to my loving wife and kids if I ceased to exist?* My mind was filled with thoughts like, *I love my life and do not want it to end,* or *I do not want to kill myself.* I wondered whether my body would survive if I killed my ego and identity. Who would I become if I did? Would I end up as a mindless or homeless person on the streets or in some mental institution? The chatter in my mind was exhausting, and in the beginning, I developed a personal hatred towards gurus, sages, and spiritual teachers (especially Mooji, Ramana Maharshi, and Nisargadatta Maharaj). My ego and personal identity hated these three spiritual teachers and convinced me to quit the pursuit of spirituality for years. You will face very similar challenges, and it is very normal. So, if you do, it's okay to feel that way, but you should know that it is your ego and personal, individualistic identity fighting the Immortal Self to self-realize. Self-realization will be the end of the transient egoistic identity, and it will fight until its demise.

It felt as if my mind was a constant chatterbox, with two fictional characters talking all day as if they were the defenders of my identity. Then, one day, I stopped paying attention to them. I thought I had the chatter under control and established that in my kingdom, there would only be one king—my Transcendent Immortal Awareness. The chatter would go back and forth like a ping-pong ball, but I remained transcendent and uninvolved, constantly witnessing the chatter, feelings, and emotions playing out on the screen of Awareness. It was a nonphysical seeing, as if from a third eye, observing the daily play of life. This detached witnessing of the play of life on the screen of my Awareness grew stronger every day, especially after meditation and contemplation.

For example, when the sensation of hunger arises in the body (the body is innocent and conditioned by habits and genetics, specially tuned for survival and reproduction), it gets bounced back and forth between the thoughts and feelings of hunger. When I identified with my primal self—as body, mind, and egoistic individual identity— signals from the body, in the form of feeling hungry, and the thoughts supporting the hunger were enough for me to attach to and identify with being hungry. As a slave to hunger, I would feed my body. However, now, as my transcendent immortal self, I remain a detached witness. My logical transcendent mind, which is very much in touch with my emotional compass, understands the interplay of feeling and thinking about hunger, knowing that my body doesn't need food but is simply engaging in habitual eating for comfort. I can calm this sensation with a drink of alkalized water. After a few minutes, when I focus my attention on writing or reading, the hunger goes away.

For a while, the chatter subsided, and my ego, along with its fictional characters, identity, and personality, seemed to fade away. But then, my ego played a different trick, creating a new personality with a messiah complex that wanted to change the world and awaken humanity. The mind and ego are incredibly resilient, capable of playing on any side of the coin if they are not caught. As Awareness, my only job was to remain as their detached witness, avoiding the traps of the mind and ego.

I remained in the unchanging sky, treating all thoughts, emotions, fears, worries, fictional characters, and imaginations as passing winds and clouds that come and go in the sky of my perception. After a while, I remained empty, detached from concepts and identity, yet I continued to act as a husband, a father, a brother, a son, a friend, a boss, and a person.

This unchanging fundamental Awareness within every human being is the Truth within us all, yet our consciousness veils it with identity, body, mind, personality, physical characteristics, and attachments. Every morning, when the brain comes to action and becomes the mind, consciousness reawakens, giving us the perception of personal identity. With this, the world emerges, and reality is created in duality. However, even in this state, I remain detached Awareness, constantly reminding myself of the true essence that witnesses my reality.

All day long, I perform the tasks that need to be done, but I never lose myself in the things of this world — identity, perceptions, duality, thoughts, feelings, and contrasting experiences. I continually remind myself who is aware of everything and who is the permanent Awareness witnessing the impermanent forms. This practice is liberating and transcendent, keeping me in a state of peace, wholeness, and joy.

As I mentioned earlier, our mother Earth is a product of our solar system, a byproduct of the Milky Way galaxy, and a tiny, microscopic cosmic dust in the universe. It has taken billions of years for our solar system and Earth to form from an extremely dense cloud of interstellar dust and gases. The process that led to this formation involved countless scenarios coming together with knife-edge precision to create perfect conditions for life to evolve on Earth. Such precision is impossible to achieve by accident without a supreme designer or creator.

Nothing complicated in this world can accidentally come into existence with such knife-edge precision. If life is an accident, then it should be possible to evolve something as simple as an iPhone accidentally. Yet even something as simple as an iPhone cannot be created by accident, let alone the complexity of life.

If you argue that a supreme designer or creator must be far more complicated than its creation, then who designed the creator? The answer is that nothing designed the creator because the creator and all of creations are One in Oneness. Human reasoning can only partially explain creation, but it can never fully comprehend the One or the Creator.

The Supreme Innate Intelligence or Creator is not a distant entity that gives birth to its creation and watches from afar. Instead, the creator is intimately involved in every aspect of its creation, manifesting new contrasting experiences and perceptions as a co-creator. Just as your awareness creates a world in your dreams full of characters, a universe, and a reality, you are both the creator and co-creator of your dream. The Creator is the Creation, Creation is the evolution, and both cosmic and biological evolution are part of the Creator, which is NoThing — birthless, deathless, boundless, limitless, formless, shapeless, and timeless, also known as Awareness.

Awareness cannot be described or named because the minute you name it or describe it, you limit the boundless, limitless, and timeless being. Everything, from particles of an atom to rocks, living beings, universes, time, and space, is made of innate intelligence —pure Awareness. Everything in creation and evolution is made of this fundamental field of intelligence and Awareness. From a particle of an atom to our universe, all are part of this fundamental invisible field of Awareness or cosmic consciousness. The more you realize this Truth, the more it reveals its mysteries to you effortlessly and with clarity.

This innate intelligence can be found all around us, in nature, from the cells of our bodies to the leaves of trees and the rising sun. It is reflected in the seasons, in the way all living things seek to grow and adapt, and in the cycles of birth, life, and death that govern all existence. It is the creative force that drives evolution, the underlying principle that brings order to chaos, and the source of all that is.

When we tune in to this Awareness, we become aligned with the natural flow of life. We move beyond the illusions of separation and recognize that we are part of something much greater than ourselves. This recognition brings peace, clarity, and a deep sense of

connectedness with all that is. It allows us to live in harmony with the world around us, to see beauty in every moment, and to experience life as a continuous unfolding of the divine.

In this state of Awareness, we are no longer bound by the limitations of the ego or the mind. We are free to explore the infinite possibilities of existence, to create and manifest our deepest desires, and to experience the joy and fulfillment that comes from living in alignment with our true nature. This is the essence of universal connectedness, the realization that we are all part of a greater whole and that our individual experiences are simply reflections of the One.

As we continue to expand our understanding of consciousness and Awareness, we will come to see that everything in the universe is interconnected. Every thought, every action, and every experience are part of a larger tapestry of existence, woven together by the threads of Awareness. As we learn to navigate this tapestry with grace and wisdom, we will find that we are capable of creating a reality that is not only fulfilling and meaningful but also deeply aligned with the highest truths of existence.

Embracing the One-ness

As you embrace this understanding of universal connectedness and the role of Awareness in all things, you begin to see the world through a different lens. You recognize that the divisions and separations that seem so real are simply illusions created by the mind. In truth, there is no separation, no duality, no division — only Oneness.

This realization brings with it a profound sense of peace and tranquility. You no longer feel the need to fight against the currents of life, to resist the flow of events, or to cling to outdated beliefs and ideas. Instead, you find yourself naturally moving in harmony with the universe, trusting in the inherent wisdom of Awareness to guide you on your journey.

In this state of Oneness, you are free to explore the infinite possibilities of existence, to create and manifest your deepest desires, and to experience the joy and fulfillment that come from living in alignment with your true nature. You become a conscious co-creator of your reality, aware of the interconnectedness of all things and the infinite potential that lies within you.

"The only way to make sense out of change is to plunge into it, move with it, and join the dance." —

Alan Watts

As you continue to deepen your understanding of Awareness and its role in the creation and evolution of the universe, you will find that life becomes an ever-unfolding adventure full of wonder, mystery, and magic. You will see beauty in every moment, the perfection in every experience, and the divine in every being. This perspective shift will enable you to approach life with a sense of curiosity and openness, recognizing that every challenge, every joy, and every sorrow is part of the grand tapestry of existence.

To illustrate this transformative insight, let me share "The Parable of the Wave and the Ocean." This parable serves as a powerful metaphor for understanding our connection to the greater whole, emphasizing that, like the wave, we are not separate from the boundless Awareness that permeates all things.

"In a distant land, there was a vast ocean stretching endlessly in all directions. The ocean was calm and serene, its surface reflecting the sky like a giant mirror. Every day, the waves danced across its surface, each one unique and beautiful in its own way. Some waves were small and gentle, while others were mighty and powerful, crashing against the shores with great force. The waves were proud of their individuality, each one believing it was separate from the others. They boasted about their size, strength, and the distance they could travel. Some waves even believed they were more important than the ocean itself, forgetting that they were born from the ocean and would eventually return to it.

One day, a small wave, feeling insignificant and envious of the larger waves, asked the ocean, "Why am I so small? Why can't I be as big and powerful as the others? I want to be important, too."

The ocean, wise and eternal, responded gently, "My dear wave, you are not separate from me. You are a part of me, just as all the other waves are. Your size, shape, and strength are temporary, but your essence is the same as mine. You are the ocean in the form of a wave."

The small wave was confused, "But how can that be? I am just a tiny wave, and you are the vast ocean. We are not the same."

The ocean replied, "Look deeper within yourself, and you will see that your true nature is not in your form but in the water that makes you. The water that flows through you flows through every wave, and that water is me. When you realize this, you will see that you are not small or insignificant. You are the entire ocean, expressing itself as a wave."

The small wave pondered this and began to see the truth in the ocean's words. It realized that it was not separate from the ocean but a part of the ocean's endless dance. It understood that every wave, big or small, was a unique expression of the same ocean and that its true essence was beyond form and size. With this realization, the small wave felt a deep sense of peace and unity. It no longer envied the other waves or wished to be different.

It flowed gracefully across the ocean's surface, knowing that it was one with the vast, infinite ocean and that every wave, including itself, was a manifestation of the same boundless Awareness. And so, the small wave danced joyfully, understanding that it was never separate from the ocean but always part of the greater whole. "

"The Parable of the Wave and the Ocean" aptly illustrates this transformative insight. Just as the wave, in its quest to understand its true nature, comes to realize that it is inseparable from the ocean, we too must recognize that our consciousness is a reflection of the greater Awareness that permeates all things. This parable beautifully encapsulates the essence of understanding that we are not separate entities but integral expressions of the same boundless consciousness.

This is the essence of universal connectedness, the understanding that we are all part of a greater whole and that our individual experiences are simply reflections of the One. As we embrace this truth, we open ourselves to the infinite possibilities of existence, and we find that life is not only fulfilling and meaningful but also deeply aligned with the highest truths of existence.

Chapter 11

The Quest for Peace Within

"The universe is full of magical things patiently waiting for our wits to grow sharper."—

Eden Phillpotts

Meditation is often misunderstood as a practice reserved for monks or spiritual gurus, but in reality, it is a tool available to everyone. It's not about escaping reality but about seeing reality more clearly. In my journey, meditation has become the gateway to understanding my true self, separating the transient from the eternal. Through regular practice, I've learned that meditation is not just sitting quietly but a process of peeling away the layers of identity that we accumulate throughout life.

The sky remains unchanging, constant, and absolute, even as clouds, storms, tornadoes, and sunshine come and go. This is how I've come to view my existence through meditation. The more I meditate, the easier it becomes to see my body, mind, consciousness, personality, attachments, dreams, and even deep sleep from a place of separation and distance. It's not like a dream but an aware, knowing, seeing (nonphysical seeing) state, like the awareness experienced during deep meditation.

Meditation has taught me that our state of mind deeply influences our perception of reality. When we are lost in thoughts, worries, or desires, our perception becomes clouded. However, when we meditate, we access a state of pure awareness where the mind is clear, and our perception sharpens. This state of awareness allows us to see the world as it is without the distortions of ego or personal identity.

Meditation, when stripped of concepts and thoughts like a newborn infant, reveals the truth within. Awareness realizes that the sense of "I am" rises from nothingness, and I repeat the mantra of "I am" within my awareness, witnessing it emerge from an empty field of nothingness. Over time, meditation becomes second nature, an unveiling of conditions, limitations, body, mind, identity, feelings, and emotions. It strips away everything learned, leaving one naked and true, like an infant, allowing for transcendence to the frequency of pure awareness.

In this state, resistance to wants, needs, desires, temptations, fears, and worries dissipates, leaving peace, joy, and contentment. Meditation isn't just sitting quietly; it's about living without the constant pull of personal identity and thoughts, existing in pure awareness, free from the constraints of the ego. It's a state of flow, whether you're a monk in deep contemplation or an athlete like Steph Curry making a perfect three-pointer. In that moment of flow, Curry is as meditative as anyone, fully engaged in the present, until the ego steps in and claims accomplishment.

The Flow State

This concept of flow—being fully present and engaged without distraction—can be seen in various fields, from athletes to artists, actors, and musicians. It's a state where one's true self merges with the task at hand, unburdened by ego or identity [36]. This alignment with the task, devoid of the distractions of the mind, allows for the purest expression of talent, creativity, and purpose. It is in these moments that we touch the essence of our being, experiencing life as it is meant to be, without the filters of past and future, without the layers of identity that often obscure our true nature.

As humanity evolved, we became conscious beings, aware of two primary worlds: one within and one outside. Our logical minds focused on the external led us to believe that everything revolved around us, creating a human-centric reality far from the truth. This belief gave rise to the notion of a dualistic God, a creator who shaped the earth for humanity in His image. Our logical minds, attached to the body and ego, lost sight of the true self, the awareness that manifests reality and experiences contrast through duality.

In this deliberate amnesia, the Creator forgets its essence in everything, manifesting as life and matter. The world we know is temporary; everything, including life on earth, will eventually come to an end. Religions speak of a Day of Judgment, where deeds determine one's

---

[36] https://www.podiumsportsjournal.com/2010/10/01/how-to-achieve-the-flow-state-inathletics-and-life/#:~:text=%E2%80%9CFlow%E2%80%9D%20is%20a%20state%20of,perform%20at %20extremely%20high%20levels.

afterlife, but I believe Heaven and Hell can be experienced on earth. By awakening to our reality, we can create Heaven or Hell here and now. We hold both angels and devils within us, and it's up to us to choose which to empower.

With awareness, you have the power to shape your reality. Believe in yourself, and you can achieve anything. The key to your success lies within you. Awareness is the key to navigating life's challenges, unlocking your true potential, and finding happiness. Consciousness, a part of the mind, body, and spirit, seeks identity, memory, experience, and perception. It craves attachment and belonging, yet it often loses itself in the game of life, detached from its roots and truth. No matter how much consciousness achieves externally—fame, money, titles—it remains unfulfilled, searching for its true essence.

When consciousness becomes attached to the body and mind, it identifies with desires and temptations, mistaking them for true presence. This illusion leads to suffering, as personal identity becomes entangled in the impermanent. Transcending personal identity, self-interest, and defensiveness is the key to overcoming suffering.

The Oneness of Existence

All things, including time, space, and matter, are impermanent, eventually dissolving into nothingness. Sir Roger Penrose explains that the end of our universe, a cold, dark, featureless abyss, mirrors the beginning before the Big Bang [37]. In nothingness, where all matter becomes shapeless, formless, timeless, and limitless lies the truth. The fundamental field of awareness manifests reality to experience itself through duality.

The death of all life forms marks the end of the mind, body, ego, and identity. Everything gained on earth is wiped away, leaving behind only the karmic memory of the soul if it doesn't transcend to a new dimension. As the universe cools and dies, new life emerges from the death of the old in an endless cycle of birth and rebirth. This cycle, driven by the laws of the universe, mirrors the spiritual journey of awakening and enlightenment. Just as the universe expands to nothingness to give birth to a new universe, our consciousness evolves, experiencing growth, decay,

---

[37] https://futurism.com/sir-roger-penrose-alternate-theory-of-the-big-bang-2

and renewal.

Sometimes, when I gaze into the night sky, I feel a deep familiarity with the cosmos, as if I've looked upon it for many lifetimes through different bodies and identities. This connection goes beyond my current existence, rooted in the awareness that guides me. It is a reminder of the vastness of existence, of the eternal journey that we are all a part of. This awareness brings a sense of peace, serenity, and belonging, knowing that we are never truly alone, that we are connected to everything, to all that is and ever will be.

When you tap into your true awareness, you access a higher reality and deeper truth. Your moral compass strengthens, guiding you with the help of your emotional compass to the right path and distinguishing good from bad. This clarity comes from living in alignment with your true self, beyond the illusions of the external world. It allows you to navigate life with confidence, knowing that your actions are aligned with a higher purpose, that you are contributing to the greater good, to the evolution of consciousness.

The Role of Behavior in Shaping Reality

John Edwards, director of CLA's School of Psychological Science, explains that our behaviors and actions shape how we experience the world. Our minds construct ideas and concepts that influence our perceptions.[38]

He further explained that in "cognitive theory, the word 'construct' explains the concepts and ideas we have in our minds. When they are activated, they are influencing us. For instance, if I have the idea of dishonesty in my mind, it's activated. It will guide my attention to the things in the environment that are consistent with or related to dishonesty, and I will interpret things in that manner"[39]. When I see someone behave ambiguously, I'll be prone to interpret it as dishonesty. But by aligning

---

[38] Arsen, D. S. (2020, November 19). Is Karma Real? Is Karma What You Think? Are Your Health and Wellness Affected by Karma? Can you Plant Positive Karma Seeds And Change Your Life!: Dr. Sarah Larsen ~ Medical Intuitive and Energy Healer. Retrieved from https://drsarahlarsen.com/is-karma-real-is-karma-what-you-think-is-your-health-andwellness-affected-by-karma-can-you-plant-positive-karma-seeds-and-change-your-life/

[39] 3August 23, 2. (2017, August 23). The Leading Edge. Retrieved from https://edge.oregonstate.edu/2017/08/23/the-science-of-karma/

with true awareness, we can break free from these constructs and live from a place of higher understanding.

Personal Reflection

As I reflect on my journey, I realize that the path to awakening is not a straight line. It is filled with twists and turns, with moments of clarity and confusion. But through it all, the guiding light of awareness has been my constant companion, leading me to a deeper understanding of myself and the world around me. It is this awareness that has allowed me to transcend the limitations of the ego, to see beyond the illusions of the mind, and to experience the true essence of existence. [40]

This journey has taught me that the key to a fulfilling life lies in the alignment of our inner and outer worlds. When our thoughts, actions, and intentions are in harmony with our true selves, we experience a sense of peace and contentment that cannot be found in the material world. We realize that happiness is not something to be sought after but something that arises naturally when we live in alignment with our true nature.

In this state of alignment, we are no longer driven by the desires and fears of the ego. We are free to live authentically to express our true selves without fear of judgment or rejection. We are able to see beauty in every moment, appreciate the simple joys of life, and connect with others on a deeper level. This is the true essence of living in awareness.

But this journey is not without its challenges. The ego, with its need for control and validation, often resists the process of awakening. It clings to old patterns, tendencies, and beliefs, fearing the unknown. But through meditation and self-reflection, we can begin to see through the illusions of the ego, to recognize it for what it is—a construct of the mind, a collection of thoughts and memories that have no real power over us.

As we continue to deepen our awareness, we begin to see the world in a new light. We realize that everything is connected and that there is no separation between us and the universe. We are all part of the same consciousness, experiencing life through different forms and perspectives. This realization brings a sense of unity and compassion, a recognition that we are all in this together and that our actions and

---

[40] Siegel, E. (2019, March 15). This Is Why The Multiverse Must Exist. Retrieved from https://www.forbes.com/sites/startswithabang/2019/03/15/this-is-why-the-multiverse-mustexist/?sh=18ee61556d08

intentions have a ripple effect on the entire universe.

Consider the profound interconnectedness of existence: our bodies are complex ecosystems, home to trillions of cells, bacteria, and other microorganisms. Each of these entities possesses its own form of individuality and potentially a rudimentary form of consciousness, contributing to the totality of our being. This idea extends beyond the individual to encompass all living beings on Earth, each with its unique identity and consciousness, woven into the tapestry of a global collective consciousness. Just as a single bacterium within us cannot comprehend the full scope and purpose of our human existence, we might also find it challenging to grasp the entirety of this global consciousness or the even more expansive universal consciousness. This analogy reflects the limitations of our understanding and the vastness of the interconnected web of life, suggesting that what we perceive is only a small fraction of a much greater reality.

From a scientific standpoint, while cells and microorganisms do not possess consciousness in the way humans understand it, they do exhibit complex behaviors and interactions that contribute to the functioning of larger organisms. These microscopic entities perform essential tasks, much like the diverse roles individuals play within the broader human society, emphasizing the importance of every part in sustaining the whole. Spiritually, many traditions speak of a universal consciousness that connects all forms of life, suggesting that every creature is a unique expression of this greater whole. This perspective encourages humility and awe in the face of the intricate and mysterious dance of existence.

This understanding of interconnectedness lies at the heart of many spiritual traditions, from Buddhism to Taoism and the teachings of indigenous cultures. It reminds us that we are not isolated beings but part of a larger whole, and our personal journey is deeply intertwined with the collective journey of humanity. By living in alignment with this truth, we contribute to the evolution of consciousness and to the creation of a more harmonious and compassionate world.

In this state of awareness, we gain the ability to see the bigger picture and understand the purpose behind our experiences, both positive and negative. We come to realize that everything happens for a reason, that every challenge presents an opportunity for growth, and that every loss teaches us the art of letting go. This perspective allows us to approach life with curiosity and openness, embracing the unknown with trust and faith, confident that the universe is always supporting us.

As we continue our journey of awakening, we may encounter moments of doubt and uncertainty. Yet, these moments are simply part of the process, reminders that we are human and still learning and growing. It is crucial to be gentle with ourselves, to acknowledge our fears and insecurities without judgment, and to offer ourselves the same compassion we would extend to a friend.

Through this practice of self-compassion, we can begin to heal the wounds of the past to release the pain and suffering that we have carried with us for so long. We can learn to forgive ourselves and others, to let go of the grudges and resentments that keep us trapped in a cycle of negativity. This process of healing is not always easy, but it is essential if we are to live in alignment with our true selves to experience the peace and joy that comes from living in awareness.

Ultimately, the journey of awakening is a journey of self-discovery. It is a process of peeling back the layers of conditioning and beliefs that have been imposed upon us to reveal the truth of who we really are. It is a journey of remembering, of reconnecting with the essence of our being, of rediscovering the infinite potential that lies within us.

As we continue this path, we may find that our understanding of ourselves and the world around us deepens. We may begin to see the interconnectedness of all things to recognize the patterns and cycles that govern the universe. We may come to understand that our thoughts and intentions have the power to shape our reality and that we are co-creators of our experience.

This realization brings with it a sense of responsibility, a recognition that we have the power to create the life we desire and that we are not victims of circumstance but active participants in the unfolding of our destiny. It is a reminder that we are always in control and that we have the power to choose how we respond to the challenges and opportunities that come our way.

In the end, the journey of awakening is not about reaching a destination but about embracing the process, about living each moment with awareness and presence. It is about finding joy in the journey, celebrating the small victories, and learning from the setbacks. It is about living with an open heart, with curiosity and wonder, with a deep sense of gratitude for the gift of life.

This is the essence of true awareness, the realization that we are not separate from the universe but a part of it, that we are not limited by our thoughts and beliefs but empowered by them. It is a journey of liberation, of breaking free from the constraints of the ego, of stepping into the fullness of our potential, of living in alignment with our true selves.

The parable of the Two Wolves highlights the essence of our internal struggle. The two wolves symbolize the conflicting forces within us— the primal self-driven by ego and desires and the true self aligned with peace and love. The outcome of this struggle depends on which aspects we nurture and focus on.

"In a small village nestled between rolling hills and ancient forests, there lived an elder known for his wisdom and clarity. The villagers often sought his guidance, trusting his deep understanding of life's complexities. One evening, as the sun dipped below the horizon and painted the sky in hues of orange and purple, a young man approached the elder with a troubled heart.

"I am in turmoil," the young man confessed. "Within me, there are constant battles between good and evil, kindness and cruelty, hope and despair. I do not know how to find peace or which path to follow."

The elder listened intently, his eyes reflecting the fading light of day.

He then spoke softly, "Inside each of us, there are two wolves engaged in an eternal struggle. One wolf is fierce and destructive,

embodying anger, hatred, and fear. The other wolf is gentle and nurturing, representing love, compassion, and peace."

The young man, intrigued, asked, "Which wolf wins this battle? How can I find peace within myself?"

The elder smiled gently and replied, "The wolf that wins is the one you choose to feed."

The young man pondered the elder's words, but his mind remained restless. Seeking further clarity, he continued, "Can you tell me more about these wolves? How do they affect our lives?"

The elder nodded and began to elaborate. "The fierce wolf thrives on conflict and negativity. It feeds on grudges, resentments, and fears. When you allow yourself to be consumed by anger, hatred, or jealousy, you are nourishing this wolf. It grows stronger, casting a shadow over your heart and mind, leaving you in a state of turmoil and unrest."

He paused for a moment, allowing the young man to absorb the weight of his words. Then he continued, "The gentle wolf, on the other hand, flourishes on love, kindness, and understanding. When you embrace forgiveness, compassion, and patience, you nourish this wolf. It strengthens, bringing a sense of calm, joy, and harmony to your being."

The young man listened with rapt attention, the wisdom of the elder beginning to resonate within him. He asked, "How can I feed the gentle wolf and ensure that it grows stronger?"

The elder's eyes twinkled with warmth as he offered guidance. "To feed the gentle wolf, you must practice self-awareness and mindfulness. Observe your thoughts and emotions without judgment, and consciously choose actions that align with your values and intentions. Engage in acts of kindness, both toward yourself and others. Nurture positive relationships and let go of negativity that no longer serves you. By cultivating an attitude of gratitude and embracing the present moment, you create an environment where the gentle wolf can thrive."

The young man, feeling a newfound sense of clarity, thanked the elder and left with a heart lighter than when he had arrived. Over time, he began to implement the elder's wisdom in his life. He practiced patience in moments of frustration, chose forgiveness over anger, and embraced compassion in his interactions with others. As he nurtured the gentle wolf, he found that his inner turmoil diminished, replaced by a profound sense of peace and contentment.

The story of the two wolves spread throughout the village, becoming a source of inspiration for many. The villagers learned that the battle within was not one of external forces but of internal choices.Each person had the power to decide which wolf they would feed, shaping their own experience of life and their interactions with the world."

By consciously choosing to feed the good wolf, we align ourselves with our true nature and foster inner peace and fulfillment. In this parable, we find a timeless truth: our inner world is shaped by the choices we make and the qualities we choose to cultivate. The gentle wolf, fed by love, compassion, and positive intentions, can transform our lives and the lives of those around us, leading us toward a path of peace and fulfillment.

Chapter 12

Living Between Two Identities

"The greatest discovery of our generation is that a human being can alter his life by altering his attitudes." —

William James.

In the journey of self-discovery, one of the most profound realizations is the existence of two identities within us. These identities are shaped by our choices, the conditioning of society, culture, religion, and even our families. Yet, it is the distinction between the primal self, the mortal, conditioned, and often misguided identity—and the true self—the immortal, transcendent, and pure awareness—that determines the quality of our lives.

When we fully grasp this, we unlock a new level of awareness. It's a state where fears, worries, panic attacks, anxiety, and depression lose their power. These feelings are just remnants of our primal conditioning—instincts tied to survival and the physical world. But when we connect with our true, transcendent self, these instincts become irrelevant. They lose their hold over us and we become liberated. The majority of all problems with humanity are caused by primal mortal identity.

Imagine living without the constant burden of fear, anxiety, and stress, without the weight of depression, without the nagging feeling of not being enough, not making enough, not having enough, and not appreciated enough. That's what this understanding offers. It's a liberation that goes beyond temporary relief; it's a lasting change in how we perceive ourselves and the world around us.

I want to ensure that this message is not just understood but felt. This isn't just for you or me; it's for anyone who reads this, especially future generations. It's a legacy of understanding that can help people in every aspect of life. Whether it's overcoming anxiety, breaking free from addiction, or simply finding peace in a chaotic world, this awareness is the key.

Reconnecting with the Primal Self

Our primal self is rooted in the physical body, the mind, and the conditioning we've absorbed throughout our lives. From the moment we are born, we are bombarded with societal expectations, cultural norms, educational and religious systems, and familial pressures that shape our understanding of who we are. This identity is often driven by primal instincts, desires, and fears—elements that are essential for survival and reproduction but can also lead to suffering if left unchecked.

The mind, shaped by natural selection to prioritize survival and reproduction, creates a veil of illusion that obscures the deeper truths of existence. The primal self—an imaginary construct of the mind— is fundamentally driven by these survival instincts. In modern times, humanity has amplified this primal drive through the sensorium, intensifying the pursuit of instantaneous gratification and further reinforcing these illusions. This gratification acts like a magician's sleight of hand, distracting us from the immortal True Self—the deeper reality beyond sensory experience. Although the mind is a product of the brain's activity, it skillfully manipulates human perception and behavior through complex and creative illusions, concealing the true nature of existence and our ultimate awareness— the True Natural Experience.

We live in a world where the primal self is often glorified. Success is measured by material wealth, physical appearance, and social status. People chase after mansions, Ferraris, designer brands, and the illusion of eternal youth through plastic surgery, all in the name of vanity. But what is vanity, really? At its core, vanity is the desire to feel superior to others. It's a pervasive affliction, affecting a significant portion of humanity. The constant need to compare ourselves to others and to feel better than our peers reflect our deep attachment to the primal, instinctual self. This instinctual self is driven by aggression, violence, resistance to change, reproduction, survival, tribalism, conflicts, competition, and selfishness. It is this primal self that fuels our desires and perpetuates the cycle of comparison and competition.

The True Self: Pure Awareness and Immortality

In stark contrast to the primal self lies the true self—a state of pure awareness that transcends the physical body and mind. The true self is immortal, unchanging, happy, and inherently peaceful. It is the essence of who we are, untouched by the conditioning and limitations of the material world.

This true self is our natural state, a state of pure awareness that exists beyond body, mind, ego, and the functions of primal self (thoughts, emotions, memory, imagination, ego, personality, and identity). It is the observer, the witness to all that we experience. When we drop everything—the conditioning, the mind, the thoughts, the imagination, the memories—we are naked and left with pure awareness, and this pure awareness is the same witness in all beings. This is the real self, the identity that we must strive to align with.

In the spiritual journey towards enlightenment, Nirvana is often likened to the purest state of being, akin to the unconditioned awareness of an infant. Here is a rephrased version of the quote, supported by spiritual texts:

"The essence of our true nature, as revealed in the attainment of Nirvana, is akin to returning to the pristine state of an infant— unadorned and unburdened by the learned experiences and acquisitions of our earthly existence. In this sacred and unblemished state, the self is liberated from the veils of conditioned existence, much like a newborn child. This true self, in its most authentic form, is devoid of the biases and judgments that shape our adult lives. It embodies a state of pure joy, boundless love, and complete wholeness, untainted by the dualities of the world."

This interpretation aligns with the Buddhist understanding of Nirvana as a state of complete liberation, where the fires of desire, aversion, and delusion are extinguished, and one's true nature is realized. It is described as a state beyond words, concepts, and dualities, transcending the limitations of the conditioned mind. In this ultimate state of enlightenment, one experiences profound peace and spiritual fulfillment, often compared to the unconditioned and unbiased awareness of an infant.

As I journey inward in meditation, I become deeply aware, yet I transcend the confines of my physical and mental egoistic self. I enter a state of oneness, where serenity wraps around me like a gentle cloak. I am bathed in pure joy and infinite love, untouched by the dualities that fracture our worldly existence. In this transcendent state, I am free, dwelling in the completeness of my true essence.

This personal reflection mirrors the core of a meditative state where I, as an individual, surpass the boundaries of my body and mind, stepping into a realm of absolute harmony and unity. It is here, in this sacred space, where the contrasts that often segment our lives fade away, and I am left with a profound sense of tranquil wholeness. In this state of Oneness, I remain as the immortal transcendent True Self, unaware of duality but fully present in the eternal Now as an infinite, shapeless, formless, boundless, and timeless Self.

The shift in perception between the immortal, transcendent True Self and the mortal, primal self is akin to the experience of observing the "Two Faces, One Vase" illusion, where one's focus can easily toggle between seeing a vase and two faces. It is a trick of the mind, powered by attention from awareness. Just as the eye can shift from one aspect of the illusion to another, so too can the mind shift its attention from the primal self to the True Self. Every aspect of our perception of this dual world is like this illusion; nothing can exist without the attention of awareness.

In the illusion, when we focus on the white color, we see the vase, representing the primal transient self that is engaged with the material world and subject to the limitations of physical existence. However, when we shift our focus to the black color, the faces emerge, symbolizing the True Self. This is the part of us that is eternal, constant, and unchanging, beyond the transient nature of our earthly identity.

This perceptual shift is effortless and can be done at will, illustrating how, with practice, earnestness, and intention, we can move our attention from the temporal and conditioned aspects of our being to the timeless and unconditioned True Self. With enough practice and the will to permanently identify with the True Self, everything becomes automatic, and the need for effort diminishes. It's a powerful metaphor for spiritual practice, where through meditation and mindfulness, we learn to navigate between these states of being, recognizing that we are truly the immortal, constant True Self while also experiencing the mortal body, mind, ego, and primal identity with its habitual tendencies.

Christ's final moments on the cross illuminate the profound truth of transcending the mortal, primal self to embody the immortal True Self. Enduring unimaginable pain, Christ did not plead for divine intervention to alleviate his own suffering. Instead, he prayed, "Father, forgive them, for they do not know what they are doing." This act of unconditional compassion and forgiveness, even towards his persecutors, reveals that Christ had transcended the limitations of the physical body and mind. In that moment, he fully embodied the realized, transcendent True Self—the essence of Christ's consciousness.

The Christ consciousness exists within every being—a state of pure awareness that transcends both the physical and mental realms, untouched by the conditioning of the material world. The True Self is immortal, unchanging, and inherently peaceful. It is the core of our being, the silent witness to all our experiences, patiently waiting for us to recognize its presence.

When we peel away the layers of conditioning—our thoughts, emotions, and memories—what remains is this pure awareness: our real self. This is the true identity we are called to align with, beyond the fleeting desires, fears, and attachments of the primal self. The primal self is driven by survival instincts and worldly concerns, while the True Self embodies limitless freedom, timelessness, and inner peace.

Christ's example on the cross serves as a profound reminder that we are more than our mortal, conditioned selves. At our core, we are the pure, eternal, transcendent True Self. By recognizing and embodying this truth, we can navigate life with grace, compassion, and wisdom. This path of self-realization allows us to transcend the limitations of the material world and align with our highest essence, leading to liberation from the stresses, fears, and anxieties that cloud our mortal existence.

This realization is not merely a spiritual ideal but a practical path to peace and unity. Christ's journey invites us to awaken to our true nature, live from a place of profound inner stillness, and engage with the world from a deeper, more compassionate understanding of our shared divine essence.

The Illusion of Primal Identity

The primal self is an illusion, a mask we wear to navigate the physical world. It is shaped by genetic programming, subconscious conditioning, and the environment in which we were raised. From childhood to the age of six, our minds are like sponges, absorbing everything around us. These early experiences form the foundation of our primal identity, leading us to believe that our thoughts, emotions, and physical bodies define us.

But this is not who we truly are. The primal self is temporary, mortal, and ultimately inconsequential. When we identify with this false self, we become slaves to our desires, fears, and addictions. We become trapped in a cycle of suffering, constantly chasing after things that will never bring us lasting happiness.

Dissociative Identity Disorder (DID)

Dissociative Identity Disorder (DID), formerly known as Multiple Personality Disorder, is a complex psychological condition characterized by the presence of two or more distinct identity states or personalities within a single individual. These distinct identities may have their own names, ages, histories, and mannerisms. The phenomenon of DID raises profound questions about the nature of self and consciousness, particularly regarding the experience of witnessing without involvement and the manifestation of distinct physical characteristics among different identities.

1. **Witnessing Without Involvement:** Individuals with DID often report a sense of detachment or disconnection from their actions and emotions. This can be understood as a psychological defense mechanism that arises in response to severe trauma, typically during early childhood. Dissociation allows the individual to distance themselves from the trauma, effectively "witnessing" events without feeling fully engaged or responsible for them. This detachment can extend to the awareness of their different identities, where one identity may observe the actions of another without feeling a sense of agency or judgment. The witness without involvement is the true self-present in the eternal, now aware of the distinct personalities created by the mind but detached and nonjudgemental.

2. **Physical Manifestations Among Different Identities:** While DID primarily involves psychological and emotional identity differences, there are also documented cases of physical variations among alters. Each altar can manifest physical variations in the same body through the focus of attention and belief while acting out the altar. This phenomenon underscores the deep connection between mind and body and the powerful influence of mental states on physical expression.

3. **The Role of Stress and Triggers:** Stress and emotional triggers can exacerbate the symptoms of DID, leading to more pronounced dissociation and the emergence of different identities. During these times, witnessing identity may become more passive, allowing other identities to take control. This can serve as a coping mechanism, allowing the individual to navigate stressful situations using the identity state best equipped to handle them. However, it's essential to recognize that all identities are mind-created illusions, with the true immortal Self remaining as the passive witness.

DID is a testament to the human mind's capacity for adaptation and survival in the face of extreme adversity. The dissociative process allows individuals to maintain a sense of safety and detachment from dualistic experiences, with more identities potentially manifesting as the trauma intensifies. Regardless of whether humans live in a single identity or multiple, we are not the mind-created delusional identity. The mind itself is nothing more than the brain in action and does not exist independently of thoughts, memory, and imagination. We are rather the constant Awareness, the detached passive witness of localized consciousness, with its attached perceptions of mind concepts and experiences of sensorium, thoughts, memory, and imagination of this mind-created identity or identities. The very same detached and uninvolved Awareness is the same One Awareness aware of different personalities in the single body and in all beings. Mind is very adaptive, creative, and illusional and can manifest individualistic identities or personalities to veil and mask the True Self.

Liberating the Soul: The Path to True Self

The key to liberation lies in recognizing the illusion of the primal self and embracing the true self. This requires a shift in perspective, a conscious choice to detach from the thoughts, emotions, and desires that arise from the primal self. We must become mindful of the chatter in our heads, the dialogues that play out in our minds, and the feelings that arise in our bodies. These are not who we are; they are simply the manifestations of the primal self.

By staying rooted in pure awareness, we can transcend the limitations of the primal self and experience true freedom. This is not an abstract concept; it is a tangible reality that can be experienced by anyone, regardless of their background, religion, or culture. The moment we realize our true self, we are liberated from the suffering that comes with identifying with the primal self.

The Benefits of Pure Awareness

The benefits of aligning with the true self and remaining in a state of pure awareness are profound and far-reaching. When we operate from this higher state of consciousness, we experience a sense of peace and contentment that is unaffected by external circumstances. Anxiety, depression, and other forms of mental suffering become meaningless, as they are merely the products of the primal self.

Take, for example, the issue of addiction. Many people struggle with addictions to substances like alcohol, drugs, or even food. These addictions are rooted in the primal self's desire for pleasure and escape from pain. But when we identify with the true self, tendencies, cravings and temptations lose their power. We can observe these tendencies and desires without being controlled by them, leading to a sense of liberation and ease.

Similarly, those who struggle with obesity can benefit from this awareness. Often, we eat out of habit or emotional need rather than physical necessity. The primal self-craves comfort through food, leading to overeating and weight gain. However, when we become mindful of our true selves, we realize that our bodies do not need as much food as we think. We can break free from the cycle of overeating and achieve a healthier, more balanced relationship with food.

Transcending the Primal Self with Mindful Awareness

Mindfulness is the practice of staying present in the moment, fully aware of our thoughts, emotions, and physical sensations without judgment. It is a powerful tool in the process of transcending the primal self and aligning with the true self. By cultivating mindfulness, we can observe the workings of the primal self without becoming entangled in its illusions.

Mindfulness, as a practice, offers profound benefits on the path to self-realization. By cultivating a state of mindful awareness, we develop the ability to observe our thoughts without attachment or judgment. This observation reveals the transient nature of thoughts— they arise and dissipate, often without any rational basis. Recognizing this impermanence is essential because it helps us understand that our thoughts do not define us; they are simply mental events passing through our consciousness.

When we extend this mindful awareness to our emotions, we begin to see them as responses to our thoughts rather than reflections of our true selves. Emotions, like thoughts, are fleeting and frequently arise from conditioned patterns of the mind. By acknowledging this, we can detach from the emotional turbulence that often dictates our reactions and behaviors. This detachment does not imply suppression or avoidance but rather a clear acknowledgment of emotions as they are, without being overwhelmed by them.

This heightened awareness enables us to step back from the drama of the primal self, the part of us driven by instinctual and conditioned responses. Instead, we can anchor ourselves in the peace and clarity of the true self, which remains untouched by the fluctuations of the mind. The true self is a state of pure awareness, a serene presence that observes without becoming entangled in the content of thoughts and emotions.

Practicing mindfulness involves techniques such as focused breathing, which calms the mind and brings attention to the present moment. By consistently reminding ourselves, "This is not me; it's my body and mind," we cultivate a healthy separation from the mental and emotional noise. This separation is not disconnection but liberation, allowing us to experience a deeper sense of self that transcends the mind and body.

With regular practice, mindfulness transforms our relationship with thoughts and emotions. Rather than being at their mercy, we gain mastery over them. Every thought, emotion, and feeling becomes a tool for deeper understanding and growth, serving the true self. This mastery brings a profound sense of liberation, as we are no longer bound by automatic reactions but can respond to life from a place of clarity and equanimity.

In essence, mindfulness is a gateway to self-realization. It helps peel away the layers of conditioned identity, allowing us to connect with the essence of who we truly are. This connection fosters inner peace, compassion, and a deeper understanding of our place in the world. Through mindfulness, we discover that our true self is not the fleeting thoughts and emotions but the timeless awareness that witnesses them.

The Importance of Identity in Human Experience

Identity is the cornerstone of our human experience. It shapes our beliefs, behaviors, and the way we interact with the world. However, the identity we choose to align with—the primal self or the true self—determines the quality of our life.

Primal identity is driven by fear, desire, and the need for validation from others. It is the source of much of our suffering, as it constantly seeks to prove its worth through external achievements and possessions. In contrast, the true self is rooted in pure awareness and is free from the need for external validation. It is content in its existence, unburdened by the fears and desires that plague the primal self.

When we identify with the true self, we experience a profound sense of freedom and peace. We are no longer slaves to our thoughts, emotions, or the opinions of others. We can navigate life with clarity and purpose, knowing that our true self is eternal and unchanging.

The Trap of Vanity and the Pursuit of Material Wealth

One of the greatest traps of the primal self is vanity—the excessive pride in one's appearance, achievements, or possessions. Vanity is a sickness, a disease that drives people to constantly compare themselves to others and seek validation through material wealth.

This pursuit of vanity leads to a never-ending cycle of dissatisfaction, as the primal self is never truly satisfied.

Consider the example of those who chase after luxury cars, mansions, or expensive clothing. These material possessions are symbols of status and power, but they do not bring lasting happiness. The primal self may feel a temporary sense of satisfaction when acquiring these things, but it is always short-lived. Soon, the desire for something bigger and better takes over, and the cycle of vanity continues.

This is why so many people with wealth and power are often unhappy. They are trapped in the illusion of the primal self, constantly seeking validation through external means. But true happiness cannot be found in material possessions. It can only be found by aligning with the true self and transcending the need for validation from others.

The Gift of Self-Realization: A Universal Experience

Self-realization is not confined to any single religion, culture, or philosophy. It is a universal experience that is accessible to all human beings. Regardless of whether one identifies as Christian, Hindu, Buddhist, Jewish, or Muslim, the true self remains the same for everyone. It is pure Awareness, existing beyond the conditioned mind and body.

The gift of self-realization lies in the realization that we are not our thoughts, emotions, or physical bodies. We are the Awareness that observes these experiences. This Awareness is eternal, unchanging, and free from suffering. It is the essence of who we truly are, and it is our birthright to experience it.

The true nature of Awareness can be seen in the emotional states of newborn infants, offering a profound blueprint for returning to our essential being. Newborns, untouched by the complexities of thought, social conditioning, or the burdens of past experiences, naturally embody a state of pure Awareness. This state is characterized by happiness, contentment, joy, wholeness, and tranquility—qualities that define our purest form of existence.

By acknowledging the transient nature of our daily experiences—our fears, emotions, thoughts, and desires—we begin to recognize them for what they are: fleeting, impermanent, and ultimately superficial. These experiences, while real in the moment, do not define us. Instead, they pass through our consciousness like clouds across the sky, leaving behind the clear, unchanging essence of Awareness.

To reconnect with this innate state, we must cultivate mindfulness and presence, allowing ourselves to remain anchored in the eternal Now. This process involves letting go of our attachment to the mind-created identities and stories that often dominate our perception of reality. By doing so, we can transcend the fluctuations of our emotional and mental states, rediscovering the inner peace and balance that reside within us.

In this reconnection with Awareness, we find a deeper sense of fulfillment and stability. Life's ups and downs no longer hold the power to sway us, as we recognize that our true nature is not tied to the external world but rooted in the timeless, formless presence of pure Awareness. This understanding opens the door to living a life that is not only more balanced but also more aligned with our highest potential, where we are free to express our true selves without fear, anxiety, or the burden of societal expectations.

The Power of Self-Realization in Overcoming Fear

Fear and anxiety are products of the primal self. They arise from the belief that we are separate from the world around us and that our survival is constantly under threat. This fear is the root of much of the suffering we experience in life.

However, when we realize our true selves, we understand that there is nothing to fear. The true self is immortal and cannot be harmed by anything in the physical world. This realization brings a profound sense of peace and freedom from anxiety.

For those who suffer from anxiety attacks, the practice of aligning with the true self can be life changing. By recognizing that the feelings of anxiety are simply manifestations of the primal self, we can detach from them and observe them without being overwhelmed. This detachment allows us to experience the peace and clarity of the true self, free from the grip of fear.

The Power of Mindset in Transforming Our Lives

Our mindset largely determines the way we perceive ourselves and the world around us. Mindset is the lens through which we view our experiences, and it shapes our responses to the challenges and opportunities that life presents. When we align with our true self, we adopt a mindset that is grounded in pure awareness rather than the limitations of the primal self.

Openness, acceptance, and a deep sense of inner peace characterize a mindset rooted in the true self. It allows us to approach life with clarity and purpose, free from the constraints of fear, anxiety, and societal pressures. This shift in mindset transforms our experience of life, enabling us to navigate challenges with grace and resilience.

How Identity Shapes Our Pursuit of Happiness

True happiness is not dependent on external circumstances or material possessions. It arises from a deep connection with our true self, the pure awareness that exists beyond the primal self. When we identify with this true self, we experience a sense of fulfillment that is not affected by the fluctuations of the external world.

Many people pursue happiness through material wealth, social status, or other external achievements. However, these pursuits often lead to disappointment and dissatisfaction, as the primal self is never truly content. True happiness is found in aligning with the true self, where we experience a deep sense of inner peace and contentment that is not dependent on external validation.

Practical Steps to Cultivate Awareness

Cultivating pure awareness is not something that happens overnight. It requires practice and dedication.

1. Mindfulness Meditation:

Spend a few minutes each day in meditation, focusing on your breath and observing your thoughts without judgment. This practice helps you become more aware of your inner world and develop the ability to detach from your thoughts and emotions.

2. Self-Inquiry:

Engaging in the practice of self-enquiry by asking "Who am I?" invites a profound exploration beyond superficial identities. This question serves as a gateway to deeper self-awareness, prompting us to look past transient aspects such as thoughts, emotions, and physical sensations, which are ever-changing and impermanent. By recognizing that these fleeting experiences do not define our true essence, we begin to uncover the constant Awareness that underlies all phenomena. This Awareness is the unchanging witness to all experiences, the silent observer that remains unaffected by the ebb and flow of life. Through persistent self-enquiry, we gradually peel away the layers of false, transient identities we have clung to, revealing the pure, detached Awareness that is our true nature. This realization brings a sense of liberation, as we come to understand that our true self is not bound by the limitations of the mind and body, but is the timeless, unchanging presence that simply is present in the eternal now.

3. Letting Go of Attachments:

To truly embark on the path of self-realization, it is essential to release attachments to material possessions, relationships, and achievements. These external factors do not define our true essence; they are transient and often lead to a false sense of identity. True fulfillment arises from within, from recognizing and connecting with our inner self. As Jesus taught, "It is easier for a camel to go through the eye of a needle than for a rich man to enter the kingdom of God" (Matthew 19:24). This profound statement highlights that the love of material wealth and the attachments it brings can obscure our spiritual vision. Jesus did not condemn wealth itself but the attachment to it, which can become a barrier to spiritual growth. By understanding that our true nature is beyond these external attachments, we can cultivate a sense of inner peace and fulfillment. This detachment allows us to experience the kingdom of heaven within, a state of being where we are aligned with our true, unchanging self, free from the illusions of the material world.

4. **Unconditional Surrender and Living in the Present Moment:**

Unconditional surrender and living in the present moment are pivotal practices in the journey of self-realization. By being fully present, we detach from the burdens of the past and the anxieties of the future, allowing us to connect deeply with our true self. Through mindful breathing—inhale for 3 seconds, hold for 3, and exhale for 6—we can anchor ourselves in the present moment, cultivating a sense of inner calm and clarity. By repeating inwardly, "I inhale peace, and I exhale primal mortal self," for a few minutes, or ideally for five minutes, we reinforce our connection to the true self. This practice helps us release the grip of the primal, conditioned mind, allowing us to transcend habitual reactions and emotional turbulence. As we breathe in peace, we invite a sense of serenity and presence into our being. As we breathe out the primal mortal self, we let go of the ego-driven fears, anxieties, and attachments that cloud our awareness. This simple yet powerful technique fosters a state of mindful detachment, enabling us to experience life from the perspective of our timeless, unchanging Awareness. This simple technique helps us surrender unconditionally to our awareness. This practice fosters a state of detachment from personal self-interest, defensiveness, conditioned habits, fears, anxieties, anger, worries, and the myriad emotions tied to the ego. By recognizing that these transient aspects do not define us, we can experience a profound sense of peace and joy. This surrender to our true self, beyond the mind and body, allows us to live more fully and authentically, embracing each moment with clarity and equanimity as nature intended.

5. Service to others:

Self-realization, a fundamental concept in many spiritual traditions and world religions, greatly amplifies our ability to serve others. By gaining a deeper understanding of our true nature, we transcend ego-driven desires and fears, allowing us to act from a place of authentic compassion and empathy. As Mahatma Gandhi wisely remarked, "The best way to find yourself is to lose yourself in the service of others." [41] This idea resonates across various religious teachings, from the Christian notion of agape (selfless love) to the Buddhist practice of seva (selfless service). Through serving others, we not only contribute to their well-being but also nurture our own spiritual growth. Self-less service cultivates a sense of interconnectedness, reinforcing the belief that we are all part of a greater whole.

Acts of kindness and support deepen our understanding of our own values and strengths, leading to a more meaningful and purposeful life. Ultimately, self-realization through service helps us align with our true nature, promoting inner peace, joy, and a profound connection to the world around us [42]. In this alignment, we discover that serving others is not merely a moral duty but a path to realizing our highest potential.

The journey to true self-awareness is a lifelong process, but it is well worth the effort. As we continue to peel away the layers of false identity and connect with our true selves, we will experience a level of peace, freedom, and fulfillment that is beyond anything the world can offer. This is a gift that we can share with others, helping to create a more compassionate and enlightened world for future generations.

Self-realization brings a profound sense of liberation as we come to understand that our true self—our Awareness—is not bound by the limitations of the mind and body. This Awareness is the timeless, unchanging presence that exists in the eternal now. Through contemplation and meditation, we ask the fundamental question, "Who am I?" and reject any answer tied to the transient and impermanent. With dedicated practice and sincerity, we begin to see that all fleeting aspects— our body, mind, ego, personality, and their functions—arise and pass

---

[41] https://theselfhelplibrary.com/the-power-of-service-finding-yourself-through-helpingothers/

[42] https://themaddphilosopher.com/2015/06/02/the-three-virtues-of-service-more-than-justdoing-what-you-love/

without affecting our true essence.

For example, if you've struggled with a quick temper, you may notice that anger arises within the conditioned mind. By observing this from a detached, nonphysical perspective, you can witness the anger without judgment, allowing it to pass without influencing your inner peace. Similarly, when thoughts or feelings of hunger arise, you recognize them as habitual responses. By shifting your attention away from these impulses, they gradually fade, leaving you in a state of stillness.

This practice of observing from a nonphysical third eye allows you to remain unaffected by the fluctuations of the mind and body. You come to understand that these transient experiences—emotions, sensations, and thoughts—do not define you; they are simply passing phenomena, observed by your true self. This realization brings a deep sense of peace and joy, as you remain rooted in your Awareness, free from personal self-interest, defensiveness, conditioned habits, fears, and desires.

In this state, you experience life from the perspective of your true self—pure Awareness, ever-present and unchanging. Detached from the body-mind complex, you find yourself anchored in a state of profound clarity, equanimity, and fulfillment, unaffected by the external world and its passing tides.

Inner peace is not something that can be attained through external achievements or possessions. It comes from within, from the realization that our true self is already complete, whole, and perfect. When we live from this place of pure awareness, we are no longer driven by the need to prove ourselves or seek validation from others. Instead, we can simply be in harmony with ourselves and the world around us.

The Parable of the Two Rivers beautifully illustrates that our primal self, driven by force and speed, can lead to turbulence and unrest in mind. In contrast, our true self, characterized by calm and balance, fosters peace and harmony.

"Once, in a serene valley, two rivers were flowing through the land. The first river, named Rina, was a powerful, fast-moving current that surged through the valley, carving out deep channels and rushing past everything in its way. The second river, called Mira, moved gently and steadily, meandering through the landscape, nurturing the land with its calm, unhurried flow. Rina was admired for its force and speed. It was celebrated for its ability to shape the land and bring dramatic changes. People marveled at its

strength and the way it carved majestic canyons. However, Rina's power came with turbulence and unrest. The force of its waters often caused erosion and chaos along its banks, and its relentless pace left little room for the surrounding life to adapt. Mira, on the other hand, was known for its serene and steady flow. It gently embraced the land, providing nourishment to the plants and animals that lived along its banks. Mira's calm waters fostered a rich, thriving ecosystem. Though not as dramatic as Rina's, Mira's presence brought a deep sense of peace and balance to the valley. The land around Mira flourished, and its gentle flow allowed life to adapt and grow in harmony. One day, a wise old sage visited the valley and observed the two rivers. He saw Rina's dramatic force and Mira's tranquil grace. The sage then spoke to the rivers. "To you, Rina," he said, "your strength and speed have created great change, but they come with disruption. Your power is undeniable, but it often leaves behind a trail of turmoil." Turning to Mira, the sage continued, "And to you, Mira, your gentle and steady flow has nurtured the land, bringing peace and balance. Your quiet strength allows life to thrive in harmony." The sage then presented each river with a small pebble. "This pebble represents a choice," he said. "For you, Rina, it symbolizes the opportunity to blend your strength with moments of calm, allowing the land to adapt to your power without being overwhelmed by it. For you, Mira, it represents the choice to integrate a bit of force and determination, allowing you to bring about change while maintaining your peaceful nature." Rina took the pebble and began to experiment with her flow, introducing moments of calm within her currents. As she did, she noticed that her power was no longer a source of constant disruption. Instead, it allowed for periods of reflection and adjustment, creating a more balanced landscape. Mira, with her pebble, embraced a touch of determination and force when needed. She found that by combining her steady flow with moments of decisive action, she could bring about changes that enhanced the valley while still preserving her essence of tranquility. Over time, both rivers discovered that their true strength lay not only in their inherent qualities but also in their ability to integrate and balance different aspects of themselves. Rina learned to blend her power with calm, while Mira incorporated determination into her gentle nature."

This is the message I want to convey: Identity is the key. By identifying with our true, transcendent self, we can overcome the problems that arise from our primal nature. We can live with peace, purpose, and joy, free from the illusions that trap most people.

I hope this makes sense. I want to ensure that this message is clear, that it resonates, and that it helps those who read it. This isn't just about theory; it's about practical, life-changing understanding. By integrating both aspects—strength and serenity—we can achieve a more harmonious existence, much like the rivers that found balance and fulfillment by embracing their complete nature.

Let's transcend the primal identity and live as our true, transcendent selves. This is the way to true liberation, to a life free from the burdens of fear, anxiety, and vanity. It's a life where we are no longer slaves to our desires but masters of our destiny.

This awareness is the key to everything. It's the foundation of a strong mindset, a healthy life, and a peaceful existence. By understanding and embracing our true selves, we can live in harmony with the universe, creating a life filled with love, joy, and purpose.

Chapter 13

The Awakening of the True Self

"We are not human beings having a spiritual experience; we are spiritual beings having a human experience."

— Pierre Teilhard de Chardin

Identifying with our True Self, the pure Awareness that lies at the core of our being, is perhaps the most significant realization one can achieve in their lifetime. This understanding is not merely an intellectual concept but a profound shift in how we perceive ourselves and the world around us. When we recognize our True Self, we begin to see that we are not the fleeting thoughts, emotions, or physical body that we often identify with. Instead, we are the Awareness that observes these experiences.

The Awakening of the True Self is not about the True Self or Awareness needing to awaken, but about dissolving the mind-created illusions that obscure it. The True Self is timeless, having witnessed the birth of the universe in the Big Bang, and will continue to witness beyond the death of time and space. It is ever-present, unchanging, and beyond the fleeting experiences of our temporal existence.

Throughout our lives, we have been perceivers through our third eye—the non-physical aspect of our being that perceives all experiences without requiring activation. This third eye exists prior to the illusory and transient personalities we adopt. Just as appliances rely on electricity to function, our experiences are perceived only through the presence of this non-physical third eye. It is the constant, unchanging witness that remains unaffected by the mind's fluctuations or the body's limitations, allowing us to see beyond the illusions and reconnect with our true, eternal nature. This awakening is a process of recognizing what has always been present—the pure Awareness that transcends all mental and physical constructs.

This shift in identification brings about a profound sense of inner peace. The mind, which is usually restless and filled with worries, fears, and desires, begins to quiet down. We no longer feel the need to control every aspect of our lives because we understand that we are not the doers; rather, we are the witness to all that happens. This realization frees us from the constant cycle of striving and suffering that characterizes the human condition.

The peace that arises from this understanding is not dependent on external circumstances. It is a deep, abiding peace that remains with us regardless of what is happening in our lives. Whether we are facing challenges or enjoying moments of joy, this inner peace remains unshaken. It is the peace that comes from knowing that we are part of something greater than ourselves, that we are connected to the very essence of life itself.

When we identify with our True Self, we begin to live life more spontaneously, just like nature. Nature does not plan or strategize; it simply unfolds according to its own inherent wisdom. The sun rises and sets, the seasons change, and life evolves without effort. Similarly, when we live from the place of pure Awareness, our actions become more spontaneous and effortless.

"And the earth We have spread out, and set therein mountains standing firm, and produced therein every kind of beautiful growth (in pairs)" –

Quran 50:7

This spontaneity does not mean that we become careless or irresponsible. On the contrary, it means that we are more in tune with the natural flow of life. We begin to trust in the process of life and allow things to unfold in their own time. This trust brings about a sense of ease and freedom that we may not have experienced before.

Living spontaneously also means that we are more present in each moment. We are not lost in thoughts about the past or worries about the future. Instead, we are fully engaged in whatever we are doing, whether it is something as simple as washing the dishes or as complex as solving a problem at work. This presence of mind allows us to perform our tasks more clearly and efficiently.

When we live spontaneously, we become more open to the opportunities and possibilities that life presents us. We are no longer bound by rigid plans or expectations. Instead, we are flexible and adaptable, ready to embrace whatever comes our way. This openness leads to a more fulfilling and enriching life as we begin to see life as an adventure rather than a series of challenges to be overcome.

Awareness as the Catalyst for Change

One of the most significant benefits of identifying with our True Self is the power it gives us to transform our lives. When we live from a place of pure Awareness, we are no longer limited by our past conditioning or beliefs. We begin to see ourselves and the world with fresh eyes, free from the filters of judgment and prejudice.

This shift in perception allows us to break free from the patterns of behavior that have held us back. We are no longer driven by unconscious habits or reactions. Instead, we respond to situations with clarity and wisdom. This transformation does not happen overnight, but rather a gradual process that unfolds as we deepen our connection with our True Self.

As we continue to live from this place of Awareness, we notice changes in all areas of our lives. Our relationships improve as we become more compassionate and understanding. We are less likely to get caught up in conflicts or misunderstandings because we can see things from a broader perspective. We recognize that everyone is on their journey and that their actions often reflect their own struggles and challenges.

Our health and well-being improve as we become more attuned to our bodies and minds. We begin to make choices that support our overall well-being, whether eating healthier, exercising more, or taking time to rest and recharge. We are more in tune with the needs of our bodies and are better able to care for ourselves.

We find that we are more inspired and motivated in our work and creative pursuits. When aligned with our True Self, we are connected to a limitless source of creativity and wisdom. Ideas and solutions come to us more efficiently, and we can accomplish more without effort. This sense of flow and ease in our work leads to tremendous success and fulfillment.

The Role of Awareness in Overcoming Challenges

Life is full of challenges, and no one is immune to difficulties and hardships. However, identifying with our True Self makes us better equipped to handle these challenges. We begin to see that challenges are not obstacles to be feared but opportunities for growth and learning.

When faced with a challenge, our first instinct may be to resist or avoid it. However, when we live from a place of pure Awareness, we are more likely to embrace challenges with an open heart and mind. We understand that challenges are a natural part of life and often hold the key to our personal and spiritual growth.

This shift in perspective allows us to approach challenges with a sense of curiosity and openness. Instead of seeing them as problems to be solved, we see them as opportunities to learn more about ourselves and the world around us. This attitude of openness and curiosity transforms our relationship with challenges and makes them less daunting.

Moreover, when connected to our True Self, we are more resilient in facing challenges. We are less likely to be overwhelmed by fear or anxiety because we know we have the inner resources to handle whatever comes our way. This resilience allows us to stay calm and centered even amid challenging situations.

One of the most profound benefits of identifying with our True Self is the ability to find meaning and purpose in our challenges. When we connect to the deep essence of who we are, we see that challenges are not random or meaningless. Instead, they are opportunities for us to grow, learn, and evolve. This sense of purpose gives us the strength and determination to overcome any obstacle that comes our way.

The Evolution of Human Consciousness: A Journey Towards Awakening

Over the years, human beings have considerably evolved in their ways. In ancient times, humans barely covered their bodies; then, they learned to cover them with leaves and flowers. Then, they learned how to sew and design clothes for themselves. This goes to show the advancement in the human brain. Human beings owe their advancement to the Atlanteans, who helped them become organized and put some fear in their hearts. How? With the help of religion. The original religion of Atlantis was sun worship.

In those days, no image of the Deity was permitted. The sun disk was regarded as the only appropriate emblem of the Godhead. The temples were gorgeously decorated, where people would come to pray to their God.

Religion gave hope. It was meant to end the sadness of the heart.

Throughout history, religions have imparted a fundamental truth: by aligning ourselves with God, we walk a higher moral and spiritual path, avoiding the chaos and suffering that arise when we stray. This divine guidance has often been framed as a safeguard against the ultimate consequence—hell. However, the concepts of heaven and hell need not be limited to the afterlife. We create our own heaven or hell in this life through our actions, thoughts, and whether we identify with our True, immortal self or our transient, primal self.

When we align with our True Self—our timeless, spiritual essence—we experience inner peace, fulfillment, and a sense of purpose: our personal heaven. In contrast, when we become overly attached to our mortal, transient nature, we are trapped in a cycle of suffering, fear, and dissatisfaction: our personal hell. Throughout history, the fear of divine retribution and the promise of reward have served as powerful motivators, guiding ethical behavior and keeping humanity's baser instincts in check.

Yet, as we evolve, we are increasingly ready to transcend the survival-driven mindset of competition and fear. We stand on the threshold of recognizing our true nature as compassionate, cooperative, and caring beings.

We are the best judges of ourselves. Reflect on how you have lived so far. You can evaluate your actions and know whether they align with your values. You don't need to look outward to decide how you've lived—everything you need is within you. By looking deep inside, you'll find the answers you've been seeking.

Religion plays a vital role in fostering unity and promoting peace among people. It offers a moral framework that helps individuals navigate life, guiding them toward ethical choices and higher ideals. The belief in both God and the devil within us reflects the internal struggle between good and evil, with faith in God strengthening our resolve to resist temptation.

One of the greatest gifts from the Divine is our innate emotional compass—a guiding force present from an early age. This compass helps us instinctively discern right from wrong, often manifesting as physical discomfort or unease when we act against our inner moral code.

This intrinsic sense of morality exists independently of external influences like teachers, books, or religious doctrines; it is a fundamental part of our being. However, if we repeatedly ignore this inner guidance, we risk becoming disconnected from it, leading to a life that strays from our true values. Religion, by reinforcing our connection to this emotional compass, plays a crucial role in preserving moral integrity and fostering a more harmonious, compassionate society. Through this connection, we are reminded to align our actions with our higher purpose, ensuring that we live in accordance with both personal and universal principles of good.

Throughout history, religion has often been misused for personal and institutional gain. Institutionalized religions have at times, distorted their core teachings to consolidate power and control, with religious leaders and scholars leveraging their influence for selfish or organizational benefits. This exploitation reveals a fundamental imperfection in humanity. In an ideal world, if everyone truly followed the core tenets of their faith, there would be no wars. Yet, peace remains elusive because humans struggle to reconcile their differences and often fail to recognize their inherent potential and the deeper purpose of their existence.

If people truly understood their divine purpose, they would see the futility of killing in the name of God, country, belief, or race. They would move beyond superficial differences and embrace the shared essence within every individual. As social beings, we possess an extraordinary capacity for connection, empathy, and understanding. However, too often, we choose conflict over peaceful coexistence. By recognizing our immense potential and our ability to form meaningful connections with others, we could transform the world—creating a more compassionate, harmonious society rooted in mutual respect and understanding.

We are capable and intelligent beings and possess the ability to be Atlanteans. You will see the power of the mind doing wonders for you. Your Awareness can help wake up that part of your brain that can help you become more intelligent.

Our race could resemble Atlanteans. All we need is faith in ourselves and our role as the co-creators. Our lives can become more accessible, better, and meaningful if we use our brains properly. The problem with humanity is jealousy and false identifications with the primal mortal self. We would be more successful if we focused on becoming spiritual beings rather than better human beings. The issue is we care about what people have to say. People judge others without any concern for their feelings. The reality is that humanity has come so far, and we can go even further.

We have evolved into strong individuals capable of taking care of themselves and others around them. We were initially introduced to the concept of law and order in the Atlantis days. People were afraid of wrongdoing because they knew the consequences. Today, we are not afraid of breaking the law. What's worse, we are not afraid of God.

The Interconnectedness of All Life: Recognizing Our Place in the Universe

One of the most profound realizations from identifying with the True Self is understanding our interconnectedness with all of life. When we see ourselves as pure Awareness, we recognize that we are not separate from the world around us. Instead, we are part of a vast and intricate web of life where everything is interconnected and interdependent.

Consider how everything is interconnected: our bodies are like miniature ecosystems, teeming with cells, bacteria, and countless microorganisms, each with its own distinct life and perhaps even a rudimentary form of awareness. These tiny life forms collaborate seamlessly to create and sustain the complex beings that we are. But this idea extends far beyond just us—it encompasses all living things on Earth, each with its own unique form of existence and awareness, contributing to a larger, global consciousness.

Just as a single bacterium within us cannot comprehend the full scope of human life, we, too, may struggle to grasp the vastness of this global consciousness—or the even greater universal consciousness of which we are a part. This highlights the inherent limitations of our understanding, reminding us that what we perceive is merely a small fragment of a much larger, more intricate reality.

This recognition of interconnectedness changes how we relate to others and the world. We begin to see that our actions have far-reaching consequences for us and the entire planet. We become more mindful of how we treat others and how we interact with the environment. We understand that the well-being of others is tied to our own well-being and that we cannot thrive at the expense of others.

This understanding of interconnectedness also brings about a sense of responsibility. We realize that we have a role to play in the greater scheme of things and that our actions can either contribute to the wellbeing of the whole or cause harm. This sense of responsibility inspires us to make choices that are in alignment with the greater good.

At the same time, recognizing our interconnectedness also brings about a sense of unity and belonging. We no longer feel isolated or alone in the world. Instead, we see ourselves as part of a larger community of beings, all of whom are on their own unique journey. This sense of unity fosters compassion, empathy, and understanding as we recognize that we are all in this together.

This realization also extends to our relationship with the natural world. When we see ourselves as part of the web of life, we become more attuned to the rhythms and cycles of nature. We begin to appreciate the beauty and wisdom of the natural world and seek to live in harmony with it. This shift in perspective leads to a more sustainable and fulfilling way of life, where we live in balance with the earth and all its creatures.

The Path to Awakening: Practical Steps for Living from the True Self

"Be still, and know that I am God" –

Psalm 46:10 (Bible)

The journey towards identifying with our True Self and living spontaneously does not happen overnight. It is a lifelong process that requires dedication, practice, and a willingness to look within. Here are some practical steps that can help you and everyone who is striving on this path:

1. **Practice Mindfulness:** Mindfulness is the practice of being fully present at each moment. By bringing our attention to the present moment, we can see ourselves and the world more clearly. Mindfulness helps us to observe our thoughts, emotions, and actions without judgment, allowing us to respond to life with greater awareness and wisdom.

2. **Cultivate Self-Reflection:** Self-reflection is looking within and examining our thoughts, beliefs, and actions. By regularly reflecting on our experiences, we can gain insight into our true nature and begin to let go of the false identities that we have created.

3. **Let Go of Attachments:** One of the biggest obstacles to identifying with our True Self is our attachment to the things of this world, whether it be material possessions, relationships, or our own beliefs and opinions. Letting go of these attachments allows us to connect more deeply with our True Self and experience greater freedom and peace.

4. **Embrace Change:** Life is constantly changing, and our ability to flow with these changes is key to living from the True Self. Embracing change means letting go of our need for control and trusting in the process of life. It means being open to new experiences and allowing ourselves to grow and evolve.

5. **Connect with Nature:** Nature is a powerful teacher and reflects our True Self. Spending time in nature helps us to reconnect with the natural rhythms of life and reminds us of the beauty and simplicity of existence. Whether taking a walk in the park, sitting by the ocean, or simply gazing at the stars, connecting with nature can help us align with our True Self.

6. **Seek Wisdom:** The journey towards identifying with the True Self is one that has been undertaken by countless individuals throughout history. Seeking wisdom from spiritual teachers, books, and practices can provide guidance and support on this path. However, it's important to remember that the ultimate source of wisdom lies within us.

7. **Practice Compassion:** Compassion is the recognition of our shared humanity and the desire to alleviate the suffering of others. Practice to be in service to others as if we are in service to Christ, Mohammad, Buddha Consciousness. In service to others and sincere unconditional humility we find our true essence. By practicing compassion towards us and others, we can begin to dissolve the barriers that separate us and experience the interconnectedness of all life.

8. **Live with Intention:** Living with intention means making conscious choices that are aligned with our True Self. It means setting goals and taking actions that are in harmony with our deepest values and desires. By living with intention, we can create a meaningful and fulfilling life.

9. **Trust the Process:** The journey toward awakening is not always easy, and sometimes we feel lost or uncertain. However, it's important to trust in the process and have faith that we are precisely where we need to be. Each step we take on this path brings us closer to our True Self and realizing our fullest potential.

10. **Embrace the Unknown:** The path to awakening is one of discovery and exploration. It requires us to step into the unknown and let go of our need for certainty. Embracing the unknown means being open to new possibilities and allowing ourselves to be guided by the wisdom of our True Self.

As you continue exploring the benefits of identifying with your True Self and living in harmony with life's spontaneous nature, reflecting on the wisdom passed down through stories is essential for you to find your True self. Parables have long served to convey profound truths in a way that resonates with our deepest understanding. One such parable that speaks to the journey of self-discovery and the realization of our true nature is The Parable of the Two Travelers.

"In a land far beyond the mountains, two travelers lived, Asha and Malik. Both had heard tales of a hidden treasure said to bestow upon its discoverer boundless peace, joy and the wisdom of the ages. This treasure was unlike any other; it was rumored to be the key to understanding the mysteries of life itself.

One day, each traveler was given a map. The maps were ancient, inscribed with cryptic symbols, poetic verses, and paths that appeared to twist and change with time. Asha, the first traveler, was a person of great discipline. She believed that the treasure could only be found by following the map with precision. Before embarking on her journey, she studied the map for days, trying to decipher its meaning. Every symbol, every line, and every curve was meticulously analyzed and recorded. Asha carried a compass, measuring tools, and a journal where she noted every detail of her journey. Malik, the second traveler, was different in his approach. He, too, valued the map, but he saw it as a guide rather than a strict set of instructions. He believed that the journey itself was as important as the destination. Trusting in the universe's wisdom, Malik set out with an open heart, allowing the journey to unfold naturally. He carried only the essentials—food, water, and a small book of poetry that reminded him to stay present in the moment. As they began their journey, the two travelers encountered their first challenge—a fork in the road. After much deliberation, Asha consulted her map and chose the most logical path according to her calculations. On the other hand, Malik stood at the crossroads for a moment, closed his eyes, and let his intuition guide him. He chose the opposite path. Asha's journey was marked by constant analysis and calculation. She measured every step, checked her bearings frequently, and meticulously documented her progress. She avoided any distractions, focusing solely on the map. Whenever she encountered a challenge—a steep hill, a dense forest, or a fast-flowing river—she relied on her tools and calculations to find a way through. Though she made progress, her journey was arduous and filled with anxiety. She feared making a wrong turn, missing a vital clue, or misinterpreting a symbol. The weight of her self-imposed expectations was heavy on her shoulders. Meanwhile, Malik's journey was vastly different. As he walked, he allowed himself to be present in each moment, soaking in the beauty of the landscapes, the birds' songs, and the sun's warmth on his face. When he came to the same steep hills, dense forests, and rushing rivers, he approached them with wonder and curiosity. He didn't shy away from challenges but saw them as opportunities to learn and grow. Along the way, he met people from distant villages, shared meals and listened to their stories. Each encounter enriched his journey, offering insights and wisdom that could never be found on a map. One day, after many weeks of travel, both Asha and Malik arrived at the entrance to a vast desert. The map indicated they needed to cross the desert to reach their final destination. True to her nature, Asha calculated the shortest possible route and rationed her supplies carefully. She set off early, determined to get to the other side quickly. Malik, however, took a different approach. He knew that the desert was vast and unpredictable, so he decided to trust in the rhythm of the land. He walked during the more excellent morning and evening hours, resting in the shade during the day's heat. He conserved his energy and water, trusting that the desert would guide him. Days passed, and the desert tested both travelers. Asha, focused on her calculations pushed herself to the brink. The relentless sun and endless dunes wore her down, and doubt began to creep into her mind. She questioned her decisions, her map, and her abilities. Exhausted and dehydrated, she wondered if she had taken a wrong turn if the treasure even existed.

Malik, though weary, remained open to the journey. He found unexpected water sources, encountered travelers who shared their provisions, and discovered oases where he could rest. He marveled at the beauty of the desert—the way the sands shifted with the wind, the colors of the sunset, and the stars that illuminated the night sky. He felt a deep connection with the land and trusted it would lead him where he needed to go. Finally, after what seemed like an eternity, both travelers reached the end of the desert. They stood before a great mountain, the final challenge before reaching the treasure. The hill was steep, with jagged cliffs and narrow paths that wound their way to the summit.

Asha, despite her exhaustion, was determined to reach the top. She studied her map one last time, tightened her gear, and began the ascent. Every step was calculated, and every handhold carefullychosen. She didn't look back or pause to take in the view. Her mind was focused solely on the summit, where she believed the treasure awaited.

Malik, too, began his ascent, but his approach was different. He climbed with a sense of reverence, pausing often to appreciate the beauty of the mountain. He listened to the sound of the wind, the birds' calls, and the leaves rustling. He trusted his instincts, allowing the mountain to guide his steps. Though the climb was challenging, he felt deep peace and contentment.

As the sun began to set, both travelers reached the summit. There, before them, lay a magnificent valley bathed in golden light. The valley was lush and green, filled with vibrant flowers, flowing streams, and towering trees. It was a place of unimaginable beauty and tranquility—a paradise beyond their wildest dreams.

But there was no treasure chest, no pile of gold, no ancient artifact. The map had led them to a place, but the treasure was entirely different. Upon realizing there was no physical treasure, Asha was overcome with despair. She had spent so much time and energy following every instruction, yet there was nothing to show for it. She sat down, exhausted and disillusioned, wondering if the journey had been worth it.

Malik, on the other hand, felt a deep sense of fulfillment. He understood that the treasure was not a material object but the journey itself—the experiences, the lessons, the connections, and the profound realization of his True Self. The valley reflected the peace, joy, and wisdom he had discovered within himself along the way.

As Asha looked out over the valley, she began to understand. The journey had not been about reaching a destination or acquiring a treasure; it had been about discovering the richness of life itself. The map had been a guide, but the actual path had been the one she walked within her own heart.

Malik turned to Asha and said, "The treasure we sought was never something to be found but something to be realized. It is the awareness of our true nature, the beauty of the journey, and the interconnectedness of all life. We have reached the treasure, not by following the map, but by allowing life to lead us to where we truly belong."

Asha smiled, tears of understanding in her eyes. She had finally seen beyond the symbols and riddles, beyond the need for control and certainty. She had found the treasure within herself—the treasure of living fully in the present, embracing the journey, and recognizing her true nature."

This parable is a profound reminder that the true treasure in life is not something external that we must chase after or strive to attain. Instead, it is the realization of our own True Self, the peace, joy, and wisdom that come from living in harmony with the flow of life. Like Malik, when we trust in the process, embrace change, and open ourselves to the present moment, we discover that the journey itself is the treasure. The challenges we face, the connections we make, and the lessons we learn along the way all contribute to the richness of our lives. By identifying with our True Self and living spontaneously, we find that the treasure we seek has been within us all along.

Chapter 14

The Foundation of Religion, Spirituality, and the Divine

"The essence of all religions is the same, only their approaches are different. In realizing the True Self, one can connect to the fundamental source of all being, finding unity in the diversity of spiritual expressions across time and cultures. The great minds of history, whether through meditation, contemplation, or intuitive insight, have tapped into this universal wellspring of knowledge, guiding humanity towards a deeper understanding of existence."

Across different ages and cultures, people have sought answers to the deepest questions of existence: Who am I? What is the purpose of life? Where do we come from, and where are we going? Despite their varied backgrounds, those who have turned inward and connected with their True Self have tapped into a universal field of Awareness that transcends all boundaries. This field is not bound by time, place, or identity, it is the source of all knowledge, imagination, and intuitive insight. It is through this fundamental field of Awareness that we access a timeless realm of understanding, where the mysteries of life unfold and where the essence of spirituality is revealed.

Throughout history, countless civilizations, cultures, and religions have independently arrived at profound truths about existence. These insights were not borrowed or copied from one another but were drawn from a shared Source—an underlying field of Awareness that transcends time and space. This universal field is the wellspring from which we access creativity, wisdom, and spiritual insight when we enter a state of flow where we are fully present and immersed in the moment. In this state, we tap into timeless knowledge, original ideas, and mystical understanding that go beyond personal experience.

Eckhart Tolle eloquently captures this idea, stating, "You are not IN the universe; you ARE the universe, an intrinsic part of it. Ultimately you are not a person, but a focal point where the universe is becoming conscious of itself. What an amazing miracle." His words underscore the profound connection between our individual consciousness and the greater awareness of the universe itself. By aligning with this field of Awareness, we become conduits for the universe's unfolding consciousness, accessing collective wisdom that has shaped human thought and spiritual insight across millennia.

To make this concept more relatable to my young boys imagine the field of Awareness as the foundation from which all creation arises, akin to a game maker who designs a complex simulation game and then enters the simulation matrix as an unbiased, nonjudgmental witness. This Awareness, devoid of attachment, identity, or consciousness (which consists of body, mind, and spirit), stays ever-present, omniscient, and omnipotent within the vast, diverse universe it has imagined. In this analogy, the game maker is the One Source, the fundamental field of Awareness. Inside the simulation room, every avatar, every piece of the universe, every thought, and every feeling exist within this Awareness. It is much like how our dreams manifest within our conscious minds while we sleep—entire worlds appear and disappear within the boundless field of our imagination. The One Awareness, therefore, is omnipotent within this simulation room, able to manifest anything from nothing, Awareness, and omniscient, knowing every thought, every intention, and every action of the avatars within the simulation. This Awareness is omnipresent in the eternal Now, not confined by time or space. Within this simulation room, everything unfolds within the One Source of Fundamental Awareness, which is Nothing—not a physical or tangible entity that avatars can see or define. It is always present in all avatars, much closer to them than the source of the imaginary identities the avatars believe they are. The avatars, the universe, and everything within the simulation matrix exists within the One Awareness, which is always aware, always aware of avatars in the game maker's simulation matrix in the waking state, the dream world, and the deep sleep state. The One source Awareness is both the subject and objects of the game, completely detached, unbiased, and nonjudgmental. In this simulation game room, avatars take their identities—shaped by culture, society, religion, politics, veils, and conditioning—very seriously. This seriousness adds drama, depth, and contrasting experiences, enriching the play of life with complexity and emotion. But to the One Awareness, it is all just a game, a neutral observation of life's play inside a simulation matrix, where nothing is gained, and nothing is lost. One

Awareness has created the simulation game with simplicity and elegance, allowing life to evolve and progress based on the fears and desires of avatars with the gift of manifestation through their fundamental powers of beliefs, imaginations, focus of attention, and surrender to Divine, who adapt to the evolutionary effects of their environments.

By connecting with this fundamental field of Awareness, we access timeless knowledge, boundless imagination, and intuitive insights that have been the foundation of all spiritual truths and religious experiences throughout history. It is from this field that the great sages and mystics have drawn their wisdom, and it is within this field that each of us can find the answers we look for beyond the confines of our perceived realities and identities.

When we recognize this field of Awareness as our true nature, we tap into a limitless source of creativity, insight, and understanding. This Awareness is the ultimate source of all inspiration, guiding us toward a deeper understanding of ourselves and our place in the universe. It is here that we realize that we are not separate from the divine but rather expressions of it, playing our roles in the grand cosmic play, each of us a unique manifestation of the One Source, experiencing the universe in our own way.

This Awareness is not tied to any single identity, race, or creed but is the timeless, boundless energy that pervades all of creation. It is the essence of who we are, beyond the masks we wear and the stories we tell ourselves. Yet, in the pursuit of power, material gain, and the endless desire to define and categorize, we have forgotten this essential truth. We have become lost in the illusions of separation and difference, forgetting that beneath it all, we are expressions of the same divine source, the One Awareness that witnesses the play of life with detachment and non-judgment.

It is a shame that most avatars on planet Earth have lost touch with their True Self, the spirit of awareness that they truly are. In losing this connection, they have also lost touch with their humanity. Throughout history and into the present day, conflicts have raged, driven by ideologies, religions, and nationalistic fervor that obscure the deeper truth of our shared existence. Consider the ongoing conflict between Russians and Ukrainians, where lives are lost over disputed territories and national pride, or the fierce and tragic struggle between Arabs and Zionist Jews, each side clinging to a narrative rooted in ancient religious beliefs and modern political ambitions. These conflicts, though seemingly different on the surface, are manifestations of the same underlying disconnection from the fundamental field of Awareness.

There are also the secret societies that operate from the shadows—unseen by most, yet wielding significant influence over the course of events on this planet. These entities are not motivated by ideology or religion, but by a relentless desire for control and power. They manipulate nations, religions, and even scientific communities to advance their hidden agendas. Their ultimate goal appears to be depopulation, reducing the Earth's inhabitants to a number more manageable under their rule.

For instance, there are rumors suggesting efforts to exacerbate tensions between Muslims and European Christians in order to spark a global conflict. This new world war, it is claimed, would decrease populations through widespread destruction and chaos. In the Western world, we also see the promotion of radical social agendas designed to fragment traditional family structures and reduce birth rates. These policies, some argue, ultimately lead to a demographic decline that aligns with the objectives of these shadowy forces.

These secret societies are not new. Throughout history, we can see their fingerprints on events large and small, always working towards the same end: control. From the Crusades, where religious fervor was weaponized to enrich a few, to the colonization of the New World, where entire peoples were subjugated and exterminated in the name of progress and civilization, these patterns repeat. But to the detached, non-judgmental One Awareness, these actions are just part of the game. The more attached the avatars in the game become to their identities, their senses, their vanity, power, money, and individualistic egos, the more interesting the game becomes. Although the game maker wants, as a detached and uninvolved witness, all avatars to wake up to the Truth within them and become the evidence of One Awareness to others, so Earth can be converted to the heaven it was originally designed for all inhabitants in One Awareness, as One Awareness.

Yet, despite the seeming chaos and division, there is evidence throughout history of a shared, deeper connection among different civilizations—a connection that transcends the physical and the visible. This connection is not a matter of shared culture or communication;

rather, it is shared access to a fundamental field of Awareness, an intelligent, aware energy that manifests in various forms of meditation, prayer, ritual, or contemplation. It is through this field that ancient civilizations, seemingly isolated from one another, were able to tap into a reservoir of timeless knowledge and wisdom, creating parallel advancements in architecture, science, and spirituality.

Consider the pyramids, for instance. The similarities between the pyramids of Egypt, the stepped pyramids of Mesoamerica, and the structures found in ancient Mesopotamia are striking. While there is no verifiable historical evidence to suggest direct contact between these civilizations, each developed a profound understanding of geometry, astronomy, and engineering that allowed them to build these monumental structures. The Great Pyramid of Giza, the Pyramid of the Sun in Teotihuacan, and the Ziggurat of Ur are all testimonies to an advanced understanding of mathematical principles and celestial alignments. Some may argue that these similarities are mere coincidence or the result of parallel evolution, but there is another interpretation worth considering: that these ancient peoples were tapping into the same field of Awareness, accessing knowledge that is not bound by time or space.

Accessing knowledge that transcends the limitations of time and space—even surpassing the speed of light—can only be achieved within the field of One Awareness. This Awareness is the sole constant, existing beyond the constraints of time and space. In this state of Pure Awareness, all knowledge that ever has been or will be, across any dimension of time and space, is eternally present in the now. This concept aligns with the understanding that Awareness is the fundamental essence of the universe—timeless, unchanging, and encompassing all possible realities.

To illustrate, imagine an experiment involving individuals from diverse cultures, beliefs, genders, and regions. If these individuals are given the same knowledge on a subject and tasked with solving an identical problem, their meditative practices, guided by awakened beings and conducted across continents—will lead to remarkably similar solutions. The differences, if there are any, would stem from societal conditioning rather than the essential truth they accessed. This phenomenon demonstrates that when we tap into the field of One Awareness, we draw from a universal reservoir of wisdom that transcends empirical evidence and individual differences, revealing the profound interconnectedness of all consciousness.

To understand this, we must look beyond the physical and the historical and consider the spiritual practices of these cultures. The ancient Egyptians, for instance, had a highly developed understanding of the spiritual world. They believed in a complex afterlife and practiced rituals designed to guide the soul through the realms beyond. Their priests were not just religious leaders but were also scholars of astronomy and mathematics, suggesting that their knowledge of the physical and spiritual worlds was deeply interconnected. Similarly, the Mayans, known for their precise calendar and astronomical observations, practiced rituals and ceremonies that were deeply tied to their understanding of time and the cosmos. They believed that by aligning themselves with the cycles of the universe, they could tap into a deeper knowledge and understanding.

In India, the Vedic sages developed profound spiritual practices, such as meditation and yoga, which were designed to quiet the mind and connect with the True Self, the Atman, which is seen as a reflection of the Brahman, the ultimate reality. These practices are not dissimilar to the meditative practices found in other ancient cultures, suggesting that there is a universal method of accessing this field of Awareness. Through meditation, individuals can transcend the physical and the mental, entering a state of pure awareness where the limitations of the ego and the senses fall away. In this state, it is possible to tap into a deeper, universal knowledge that is not bound by time or space.

Modern examples of this phenomenon can also be found. Consider the cases of Thomas Edison and Nikola Tesla, two of the most brilliant minds of the 19th and 20th centuries. Edison was known for his ability to enter a hypnagogic state—a state of consciousness between wakefulness and sleep—where he could access flashes of insight that led to some of his most famous inventions. Tesla, on the other hand, was known for his ability to visualize his inventions in perfect detail, often stating that he received these visions fully formed.

Both men, in their own ways, were tapping into a field of Awareness that allowed them to access knowledge and insights beyond the ordinary.

These examples, both ancient and modern, suggest that there is a common denominator in human experience, a fundamental field of Awareness that is accessible to all who seek it. This field is not limited by time, space, or identity; it is the source of all knowledge, imagination, and intuitive insight. It is through this field that we are all connected, regardless of our backgrounds, our beliefs, or our circumstances. And it is through this field that we can find the answers to the deepest questions of existence, not by looking outward, but by turning inward and reconnecting with our True Self.

Throughout history, the rise and fall of civilizations have often been accompanied by periods of great spiritual awakening, where individuals and groups have sought to reconnect with this field of Awareness. The Renaissance in Europe, for example, was not just a period of artistic and scientific advancement but also a time of spiritual exploration and renewal. The works of Leonardo da Vinci, Michelangelo, and others were deeply influenced by their understanding of the divine and their desire to express this through their art. Similarly, the Enlightenment, which followed, was not just a period of reason and scientific discovery but also a time when thinkers like Isaac Newton and Gottfried Wilhelm Leibniz sought to understand the divine order of the universe through the lens of mathematics and science.

In more recent times, the spiritual awakening of the 1960s and 1970s, often referred to as the New Age movement, saw a resurgence of interest in meditation, yoga, and other spiritual practices. This period was marked by a desire to reconnect with the True Self and explore the deeper dimensions of existence. The writings of figures like Alan Watts, Ram Dass, and others helped to popularize these ideas, encouraging a new generation to seek answers beyond the material world.

Yet, despite these periods of awakening, much of humanity remains disconnected from their True Self, lost in the illusions of the ego and the material world. The conflicts and divisions that plague our world today are a reflection of this disconnection, a symptom of a deeper spiritual malaise. The wars, the violence, the hatred—all of these are manifestations of a lack of awareness, a failure to recognize the fundamental unity of all life.

In much the same way that ancient spiritual seekers would retreat into nature or solitude to commune with the divine and find answers to the mysteries of existence, modern minds like Edison and Tesla found their own paths to the universal source of knowledge. When Thomas Edison hit a wall with his inventions, he didn't turn to books or external advice; instead, he turned inward. By sitting in his armchair, holding a steel ball, and allowing himself to drift into a hypnagogic state, Edison accessed a deeper layer of consciousness. As his muscles relaxed and the ball dropped, he would wake up with insights and revelations about his problems. This method wasn't about hard work or grinding effort—it was about letting go, about quieting the mind enough to let the answers come from a place beyond ordinary thought.

Nikola Tesla, too, understood the power of this inner world. He developed a practice of visualization that went beyond mere daydreaming. In his mind's eye, he could see, feel, and manipulate his inventions as though they were already real. Tesla's ability to visualize complex machines in perfect detail and test them in his imagination came from his understanding that the universe operates on principles of energy, frequency, and vibration. He believed that by aligning himself with the frequency of universal intelligence, he could receive any knowledge he sought. Tesla knew that to truly connect with this frequency; one must strip away all learned behaviors, beliefs, and identities, everything that ties us to the material world. He spoke of becoming an "unveiled energy," a pure, naked awareness that can tap into the boundless potential of the cosmos.

"Do not be deceived by the light of the day," he might have shared my idea, "because True beauty and mysticism are in the darkness of the night." In the stillness and silence of the night, in the absence of external distractions, one can turn inward and discover the universe within. "Do not be deceived by man and book worshipers because God worshipers realize the Truth from the soul of any newborn infant." An infant's soul, untainted by the conditioning of society, holds the purity and clarity that most adults lose as they grow older. It teaches us to love unconditionally, to hope and have courage, to find joy in simplicity, and to accept all without judgment. An infant knows, without words or concepts, the unity of all things. It is a living testament to the idea that the cosmos is within us all.

"Do not be deceived by your body, mind, and ego," for these are mere constructs, temporary vessels for the eternal awareness that we truly are. The path to true freedom and peace lies in following your soul's compass, a divine guide that resides within each of us. When you learn to listen to this inner voice, you will never be lost. You will find that you are already free in essence, that you can witness the experiences of this life without becoming entangled in desires, judgments, or fears. In this state of pure awareness, you will taste heaven on earth.

This is the wisdom I wish to pass on to my children and anyone who is open to hearing it. It is a universal knowledge, accessible to all beings if they are courageous enough to "kill" themselves in the spiritual sense— letting go of the ego, the mind, the conditioning, the limitations, and the thoughts that make up the personality. To truly live, one must transcend the small self before physical death, discovering the power of being one with the Oneness of all things.

"Be empty as a vast, boundless, silent, intelligent space," witnessing all that happens within and around you without attachment or judgment. Surrender to the Universe, and you will find that everything aligns for your highest good. When you are empty of thoughts, emotions, feelings, identity, and persona—when you are devoid of all that changes—you become a vessel for Grace. You will say the right thing, see the truth, be in the right company, and find yourself in the right place. This is not a matter of chance but a natural result of synchronicities and being aligned with the universal flow.

In this state, you remain as your True Self—the permanent perceiver of perceptions, the witness of the body, mind, and the happenings of life. Practice surrendering to the will of God, becoming utterly empty within, even if just for a week, and you will feel lighter and more peaceful. Your greatest power lies in your belief and the focus of your attention. Know this strength and focus only on your True Self. When thoughts trouble you, engage in activities that bring joy and release, such as singing aloud, dancing wildly, or jumping on a trampoline. Meditate, and before you sleep each night, repeat to yourself, "I love you and appreciate you, God, for all the blessings in my life, for my breath, body, mind, and contrasting experiences. Thank you, Universe, for transcending me to be aware of this body, mind, ego, personality known to me as (your name) Rameen Zereh. Thank you, God, for transcending me to identify as Universal Awareness" Continue this practice until all thoughts, feelings, and emotions fade away, and you remain in a state of emptiness, resonating with the frequency of Pure Awareness.

You are not just the body and mind you experience; you are the one who watches, the silent observer witnessing all comforts, pleasures, emotions, discomforts, and experiences without attachment, prejudice, or judgment. We are the Universe, and the Universe is within us. Look to the cosmos, "which tells us that the chemical elements of life—hydrogen, oxygen, carbon, and nitrogen—are the most common elements in the universe. We are not simply in the universe; the universe is in us. Understand this, and you will see that every being in this universe is one with the Oneness of all existence" Neil deGrasse Tyson.

It's time we transcend the small-minded and personal view of life, seeing beyond the limitations of our bodies and minds, and recognize our interconnected greatness. As I walk around Lake Merritt in Oakland, witnessing homelessness, addiction, and despair, I am filled with a deep longing to awaken everyone to their own inherent greatness. If only they could see beyond their self-imposed limitations and understand the boundless potential within. Yet, I realize this understanding cannot be imposed; it must arise from within. Speaking of such truths often invites skepticism and accusations of delusion, but I know it in my heart to be the Truth. I see One Awareness shining through the individual filters of our personal experiences, identities, and egos. The Divine play invites us to embrace our interconnectedness and awaken to the Truth that resides within each of us.

I have the power to change only myself and the courage to become the evidence of this truth through my actions. By transforming my own identity, ego, body, and mind, I can become a beacon of truth to those around me. Every human being has the potential to transcend their conditioning and limitations to become the evidence of Truth in this life.

In our existential quest, we stand at the crossroads between the True Self and the primal mortal self. The True Self is akin to an eternal essence, devoid of shape, mind, color, or form, bound by neither time nor mortality. This Pure Awareness is the source of all manifestations; it is the origin and return point of everything physical, quantum, and metaphysical. Imagine looking at your hand before your eyes—ask yourself, who is aware of perceiving the sight of your hand? Your attention, rising from Pure Awareness, focuses on the act of seeing, making your hand and the act of seeing the objects of your experience, while the perceiver remains the subject. This Pure Awareness is beyond all forms and identities; it is a transcendent state of being, intrinsically immortal and pure. When we identify with this True Self, we experience a profound sense of lightness, happiness, joy, contentment, and equanimity—an unshakeable state of being that remains untouched by the transient nature of the physical world. Before we mask it with shapes, forms, colors, identities, personalities, and ego, this Pure Awareness shines as the One in all beings, ever present and ever-aware.

Conversely, the primal mortal self is the embodiment of our physical existence—encompassing the body, mind, ego, personality, and individual identity. This self is finite, subject to the limitations and sufferings of life. When we identify solely with this aspect of our being, we become vulnerable to the burdens of existence, manifesting as fear, worry, anxiety, problems, and misery.

Transcending the karmic, genetic, subconscious, and conscious memories is akin to placing a glass full of red wine under a faucet and allowing clear, clean water to flow into it. Gradually, the water dilutes the wine, and eventually, the dark wine is replaced by pure, transparent water. Similarly, when we practice mindfulness and awareness, we slowly transcend the pulls of our body and mind—our tendencies, habits, addictions, thoughts, feelings, emotions, and sensations. Our True Self often becomes obscured by the conditioning and tendencies of our body, mind, ego, identity, subconscious, and genetic layers—veils that hide the immutable truth of who we are beneath transient, illusory experiences.

Through the practice of mindfulness—watching the 'traffic' of thoughts and emotions without attachment or judgment—we begin to dissolve these layers. By remaining detached and uninvolved, we allow the comings and goings of life to pass by without affecting our core essence, which remains serene and untouched. This process liberates us, enabling us to experience pure awareness and perceive everyone and everything for what they truly are. As we cultivate mindfulness and awareness, we transform, gradually transcending these veils, revealing the clear, unchanging True Self within.

To truly understand the nature of reality, we must go beyond the surface and explore the deeper dimensions of existence. We must learn to see the world through the eyes of Awareness, recognizing that all our experiences, all of our thoughts and emotions, are manifestations of a deeper, underlying reality. It is only by reconnecting with this reality, by remembering our True Self, that we can begin to heal the wounds of the world and create a future where all beings can live in peace and harmony.

As we look to the future, it is clear that the challenges we face are great. Climate change, social inequality, racism, phobias, economic inequality, political instability—these are just a few of the issues that threaten our world. But these challenges are not insurmountable. They are not a reflection of a broken world but of a world that is in the process of waking up, of remembering its True Self.

The path forward is clear: we must transcend the illusions of the ego and reconnect with the fundamental field of Awareness—the source of all knowledge, creativity, and intuitive insight. This True Awareness has been the origin of all wisdom, inventions, and insights throughout history, and it will continue to guide humanity. Writers, artists, inventors, and creators serve as conduits, channeling this universal Awareness through their high emotional and intellectual capacities. To tap into this flow, we must embrace practices such as meditation, prayer, and contemplation—time-tested methods passed down through generations. We need to live in harmony, recognizing that we are all expressions of the same divine Awareness, each contributing to the grand tapestry of existence.

Imagine a society where leadership emerges from the grassroots. In this community, everyone lives in equality, serenity, and freedom, with leadership roles open to all who embody universal values and long-term wellbeing.

This society values active participation, creativity, and shared purpose. Leaders are chosen through collective consensus based on wisdom, integrity, and commitment to the common good.

Political systems are transparent and inclusive, with decision-making processes that involve local populations. Policies focus on sustainability, social justice, and the well-being of future generations.

Economically, fairness and equity are prioritized, ensuring basic needs are met for all. Social enterprises and cooperatives reinvest profits into the community, and financial systems support ethical investments and green technologies.

Education is holistic, promoting intellectual, emotional, and spiritual growth, with an emphasis on collaboration, mindfulness, and environmental stewardship.

In essence, this society embodies unity, freedom, minimal government intrusion, shared universal purpose, and mutual respect, fostering a culture of inclusivity and empathy, where personal fulfillment and universal collective well-being are intertwined and aligned.

As I reflect on the wisdom of the ancients, I am particularly drawn to the parable of the lost coin. It serves as a poignant reminder that sometimes, when we are searching for something valuable, we can become so fixated on the object itself that we overlook the simple solutions right before us. Just as the woman in the story needed to create better lighting to find the coin, we may need to adjust our perspective or approach to uncover what we truly seek.

"A woman lost a valuable coin in her house. She searched high and low, turning over furniture, checking under rugs, and even looking behind curtains. Despite her best efforts, she couldn't find the coin. Exhausted and discouraged, she sat down on the floor and began to weep. In her despair, she remembered a wise old woman who lived nearby. She went to the woman's house and explained her situation. The wise woman listened patiently and then said, "My dear, instead of searching for the coin, why don't you light a candle and sweep away the shadows?" The woman was puzzled by the wise woman's advice, but she followed it. She lit a candle and swept away the shadows in her house. As she did so, she noticed a glint of light under a piece of furniture. She moved the furniture, and there, in the light of the candle, she found the lost coin. "

The parable of the lost coin teaches us that sometimes when we're searching for something, we need to change our perspective. Instead of focusing on the object of our search, we should look for conditions that might make it easier to find. In this case, the woman needed to create better lighting to see the coin.

In this dance between the True Self and the primal mortal self, the choice is always ours. We can choose to be bound by the transient, ever-changing experiences of life, or we can choose to align with the eternal, unchanging essence of our True Self. The path to awakening lies in this choice, in the willingness to see beyond the illusions of the physical world and embrace the oneness that connects us all. By doing so, we not only find peace within ourselves but also become a source of peace and awakening for others.

Conclusion

Ultimately, my heartfelt plea is for no one, especially my descendants, to hold onto the words of this book or any text as absolute truth. Every written work reflects someone's understanding and concepts of their own Truth and serves as a guidepost toward discovering your own. Instead, I encourage an inward journey through contemplation and meditation, aligning with the flow of your authentic essence. In this state of harmony, pose your deepest questions, trusting that the universe will reveal the answers—without the need for entheogens, mysticism, or magic. All written knowledge, past and future, resides in the field of Awareness and is accessible once you resonate with your True Self. As your dedication to contemplation deepens, so too will the mysteries of the universe unfold before you with increasing clarity. The right energy, frequency, and vibration are necessary for asking meaningful questions and comprehending the answers.

Consider the contrast between Newtonian and quantum physics. Newtonian physics relies on deliberate actions—gathering knowledge through books, absorbing it, and then applying it. Quantum physics, however, suggests that by embodying the energy, frequency, and vibration of your desires, you naturally align with them, drawing them toward you. There is no need to traverse time and space; simply becoming one with the essence of your aspirations allows them to manifest in your reality.

When you meditate and transcend the limits of your body, mind, and identity, you connect with pure Awareness. In this state, knowledge and wisdom flow to you directly from the universe. This Awareness is not bound by time or space, granting you the ability to access information instantaneously. All knowledge exists in this eternal present moment.

Imagine an experiment where individuals from diverse backgrounds are given the same problem. Through meditation and contemplation, guided by enlightened beings, they arrive at similar solutions, even when separated by vast distances. This illustrates that by tapping into universal Awareness, we access shared wisdom that transcends individual differences, highlighting our deep interconnectedness.

This book may serve as a guide for those advanced on their spiritual journey, offering insights into further evolution. Conversely, it may be unsettling for those deeply rooted in materialism or egocentric pursuits. I advise you against reading this text if you are struggling with psychological challenges or if your focus is on personal gain. It is particularly unsuitable for those who haven't reached the spiritual maturity needed to appreciate the wisdom behind Rumi's words: "You must die before you die." Let those who are not yet ready pause here. Only when you are prepared should you continue, engage in deep meditation, and embrace the Oneness that connects us all.

How can you know if you're ready? The answer is clear. Those who are not ready will feel resistance, anger, hate, or the urge to criticize. They will disregard the underlying message and focus on critiquing the tone, style, and references of my book. Those ready will feel a strong urge to pursue self-realization to find unconditional happiness.

For those not yet ready, I plead with you to stop reading this or any other spiritual text. Your egoistic identity may attract disease to your mental and physical well-being. Those called to proceed must understand that to uncover the True Self, the ego, personality, identity, and primal self must be relinquished.

The secrets of the universe are revealed through surrender to the Divine. In times of uncertainty, I recite the mantra: "There is no cause and effect; everything is preordained. I am a small character in this book written by Divine. I surrender to life's spontaneous unfolding potential, and there is no need to force, resist, or manipulate anything or anyone. I let go of all self-interest, self-defensiveness, fears, and anxieties, and the ego known as Rameen Zereh. Thank you, God, for transcending the primal mortal self to remain as True immortal Self, the constant Awareness." This practice has deepened my connection to the universe and brought me contentment and peace.

Shifting my focus from the mortal self to the True immortal Self has liberated me from worldly stress and unnecessary fears. This shift alleviates anxiety, depression, addictions, and even societal issues like violence and inequality. The Divine, like the sun shining impartially, can illuminate the heart of anyone, regardless of race, gender, culture, or politics.

Letting go of old beliefs, even temporarily, requires an open heart.

This process is akin to awakening from a dream into a lucid dream, where you become aware of the dream and of your awareness within it. When I rest in my Awareness and identify as the immortal True Self, I observe life's movements, like clouds drifting across the sky. If I wish to engage, I simply focus on one and descend to play within it as my mortal self.

In this state, the primal self is no longer an obstacle but a tool under my control, serving a purpose in this existence. It enables us to experience joy—chocolate, flowers, love, and the beauty of life. Shifting attention between the primal self and the True Self becomes effortless, a natural and simple act. There is no need for mysticism or magic to access this realization, as it is our inherent nature, often overlooked. The shift is as simple as choosing between two images in the mind's illusion—like seeing both the vase and the faces in the famous optical illusion.

To illustrate, consider the lotus flower. It rises from muddy water yet blooms pure and beautiful. Similarly, our True Self can emerge from the murky depths of our primal existence, untouched and radiant. Or think of the sun obscured by clouds. The sun always shines, just as our True Self is ever-present, while transient thoughts and emotions are the clouds that come and go.

By embracing these spiritual truths, we can navigate life with ease and grace, recognizing our eternal essence even as we engage with the shifting experiences of the mortal self.

Though it may seem mystical or elusive, the realization that we are the shapeless, timeless, and limitless True Self—known as Awareness—is attainable for all. As I increasingly identify with this True Self, the Divine light illuminates my third eye, allowing me to perceive beyond physical senses. I become aware of seeing without eyes, hearing without ears, and being without the limitations of the body. In this heightened Awareness, everything around me serves my True Self, which reigns sovereign.

As I transcend dualistic perceptions, I remain in the Oneness, free from emotional, psychological, and worldly challenges, in a state of peace. This profound shift is not just spiritual awakening—it is liberation from the confines of the mortal self. The problems of the world, from anxiety and addiction to societal issues, dissolve as I rest in the essence of my

True Self, eternally at peace.

Rising Above the Illusions of the Mind

The mind, with its complex network of thoughts, emotions, beliefs, and perceptions, often creates a dualistic view of reality, dividing the material from the spiritual and the self from the other. Yet, this separation is merely an illusion—like the famous optical illusion of two faces that also form a vase. Just as focusing on different aspects of the image reveals new forms, shifting our awareness can unveil the deeper nature of reality. With dedication and practice, one can transcend these mental illusions. Techniques such as mindfulness, meditation, compassion, selfless service, and self-inquiry quiet the mind and peel away layers of conditioned thinking, gradually uncovering the core of pure awareness.

In this elevated state of awareness, the material world and dualistic perceptions are recognized as projections of the mind. Everything arises within awareness, the fundamental essence of all existence. The material and spiritual are not separate; they are different expressions of the same underlying reality. This realization requires neither mysticism nor supernatural powers—it is the natural state of being, often overlooked due to the mind's distractions. Just like an optical illusion, it is as simple as shifting attention. By turning inward and recognizing awareness as the foundation of all, one can experience the unity that exists beneath the surface of all things.

Consider the analogy of lucid dreaming. In a lucid dream, the dreamer knows they are dreaming and can see the dream world as a creation of their consciousness. Similarly, in the waking state, one can realize that the material world arises from the mind within the field of awareness. This awareness is the true self, the essence that transcends the mind's illusions. By rising above these illusions, one experiences the profound truth that everything is one. The material and spiritual, the self and other—all emerge from the same awareness. This realization dissolves duality and reveals the interconnectedness of all existence. It is a return to the essence of who we are, where the boundaries of duality fade, and the true nature of reality is revealed as pure awareness.

Spiritual journeys often begin with a seed of belief, acting as a catalyst to open the mind to realms beyond the material world. As one delves deeper, experiences like lucid dreaming may emerge, blurring the lines between the conscious and subconscious, offering glimpses into deeper layers of the True Self.

The parable of wise traveler offers insight into transcending mind illusions and staying detached as the True Self. A wise traveler arrived at a magical train station where each train symbolized different life aspects.

A luxurious train with enticing aromas of delicious food and wines arrived, but the traveler remained on the platform. Then, a lively train with laughter and music came, yet the traveler stayed grounded. An angry train followed, filled with shouting, rude, angry, and hateful passengers, and still, the traveler stayed detached, observing the chaos.

Different trains came all day, representing desires, fears, aversions, and temptations, but the wise traveler resisted boarding, understanding they were mere illusions. Initially, it was challenging to stay, but over time, the temptations lost their power.

Eventually, the traveler realized that life's journey can be witnessed from a place of inner stillness, happiness, and peace. By staying on the platform of Awareness, the traveler found sanctuary from the mind's constant chatter, hustle, and chaos. The traveler continued their journey from the serene platform of their true Self, observing life's comings and goings with a tranquil heart.

Confronting the Primal Mortal Self

Through primal bodily and mental experiences, we encounter the primal mortal self—the aspect tied to physical existence, instincts, and ego. This realization is essential, as it grounds us in our human experience, acknowledging our limitations and vulnerabilities. The primal self, driven by competition, tribalism, jealousy, and selfishness, is an evolutionary survival mechanism focused on the sensorium and external world.

As we recognize the influence of the primal mortal self, we begin to understand our habits, instincts, and reactions. This awareness allows us to acknowledge their purpose in survival while learning to detach and transcend them. By doing so, we move toward a state of greater mindfulness, aligning with our True Immortal Selfless Self.

Differentiating: Primal Mortal Self vs. True Immortal Self

As the journey unfolds, a clear distinction emerges between the primal mortal self and the true immortal self. The true self transcends physical existence, embodying timelessness and boundless awareness. This differentiation marks a pivotal moment, shifting focus from transient identities to the eternal essence. Here, we have a choice: remain tranquil in the True Immortal Self or engage with the transient aspects of life, becoming a participant in the divine play.

Illumination: Unified Reality

In this state of heightened awareness, a profound truth emerges: the material and spiritual worlds are not separate but are expressions of a unified awareness. Duality dissolves, revealing that everything— objects, perceptions, and experiences—is interconnected and rooted in pure awareness.

The Aware Universe

From both a scientific and spiritual perspective, this journey highlights the interconnectedness of all things. Matter, dark energy, space, and time are not isolated phenomena but are intertwined within the fabric of awareness. The entire universe is a manifestation of this pure awareness, where the material and spiritual converge into a harmonious whole.

This understanding invites a holistic view of existence, where the journey through belief, lucid dreaming, and self-realization is a path to grasping the true nature of reality—an aware universe in which everything arises from a single awareness, akin to the world we create in a lucid dream.

Final Words

As we come to the close of this shared journey, I hope the insights within these pages have acted as signposts, guiding you from merely pondering the nature of existence to truly experiencing its boundless depth. Life is a grand, Divine play—a dance where we are invited to revel in heaven on earth, immersed in its contrasting diversity and breathtaking beauty. Each moment is a chance to embrace the wonders around us, to find joy in the simple and the profound.

But remember, while we delight in the experiences of the senses, there comes a time to transcend them, to look inward and realize the Truth that has always resided within. This journey is about moving beyond intellectual understanding, awakening to the reality that your true, immortal, selfless essence exists before all else. It's about recognizing that the entire universe unfolds within your awareness.

The path to self-realization might have its challenges, moments sprinkled with uncertainty and doubt. Yet, take heart in knowing you are not walking it alone. I'm here beside you, ready to guide and support, to ease any burdens when they feel heavy. Together, we can navigate the twists and turns, moving toward a deeper understanding of our true selves.

If ever the journey feels overwhelming, don't hesitate to reach out. Let me lend a hand, a word of encouragement, a shared smile. Let's continue this adventure together, embracing the Divine play of life with open hearts and cheerful spirits. May you find peace in the stillness within, joy in every step, and clarity in the realization that you are both a participant and a witness in this magnificent tapestry of existence.

Here's to celebrating the fullness of life, transcending beyond the sensory, and awakening to the boundless Truth that shines from within you.

Throughout history, humanity has sought the profound truth of Self-realization through diverse spiritual traditions and practices. Whether one embarks on this sacred journey via Eastern spirituality, indigenous rituals, Sufism, Gnostic Christianity, or Kabbalah, the ultimate destination is still the same: the realization of the One True Immortal Self.

In our modern age, countless resources are available on platforms like Audible, eBooks, and YouTube to aid in this quest. Immersing oneself in the teachings of revered spiritual masters such as Saint Francis of Assisi, Shams Tabrizi, Nisargadatta Maharaj, Ramana Maharshi, Rumi, Rabbi Isaac Luria (The Ari), Laozi, Buddha, Black Elk, Maria Sabina, Al-Ghazali, Hazrat Inayat Khan, Valentinus, Rabbi Isaac Luria (The Ari), Mother Teresa, and last but not least my teacher Mooji can be particularly transformative. Engaging with their wisdom during meditation, upon awakening, and just before sleep can deepen one's experiential understanding. Create an audible from any teaching that touches your heart and plays the audible when your subconscious mind is most receptive during meditation, before falling asleep, and right after waking from deep morning sleep.

Self-realization transcends cultural, religious, societal, and group boundaries. It is a universal journey, accessible to all beings, leading to the experiential knowing of our true nature. This path, though varied in its expressions, converges in the timeless truth of our shared essence.

Let us embark on this extraordinary journey with open hearts and joyful spirits. Never hesitate to seek the guidance of an awakened master, and trust your intuition as you select the teacher who resonates with you. I wish you serenity in your quiet moments, happiness in each stride, and clarity in realizing that you are both engaged in and witnessing the remarkable fabric of life. Let us honor the gift of existence, rise above the physical realm, and uncover the profound Truth that resides within you.

Embracing this journey is a truly remarkable path, filled with boundless happiness and deep contentment.

It is essential to explore the profound practice of meditation, which involves emptying oneself of thoughts, memories, imagination, emotions, and feelings. This process, akin to resetting the mind, allows us to return to a state of innocence—like a newborn, free from the layers of conditioning, limitations, beliefs, wants, needs, temptations, addictions, and the accumulated identity of a lifetime.

In this meditative state, strive to remain absolutely formless, shapeless, birthless, deathless, and timeless—as pure Awareness. This concept transcends both the physical and mental realms, reaching the very core of our existence. The body, in its natural state, operates with an innate intelligence—an intrinsic wisdom that governs its functions regardless of the mind's influence. Even in cases of amnesia, where personal identity is lost, the body continues to function, waking each day, breathing, and performing autonomic processes effortlessly. This highlights the profound intelligence within our physical form, independent of our conscious awareness.

Consider the notion of dissociating from your personality, identity, and even gender. This dissociation doesn't negate the importance of these aspects but rather emphasizes the underlying reality that our bodies operate seamlessly, surrendered to this internal, innate intelligence. This intelligence is not confined by the constructs of self we typically identify with—names, professions, roles, or even the distinctions of male and female. Instead, it is an expression of a deeper, universal Awareness that transcends individual characteristics.

Engaging in this meditative practice, we allow ourselves to step back from the incessant chatter of the mind and the emotional turmoil of our daily experiences. We begin to witness the transient nature of thoughts and feelings, understanding that they do not define our true essence. By cultivating this state of pure Awareness, we tap into a sense of tranquility and equanimity, realizing that at the core, we are timeless beings connected to a greater whole.

This practice fosters a profound understanding that our true Self is not bound by the ephemeral conditions of the physical world but is an enduring presence that observes and experiences life without attachment. It is a journey inward, to a place where we can reconnect with the essence of our being, finding peace and purpose beyond the illusions of ego and the material existence. In this state of pure Awareness, we can navigate life with greater clarity, compassion, and insight, recognizing the inherent unity of all existence.

Meditation Script: Embracing the True Self

Find a quiet place where you won't be disturbed. Sit comfortably and close your eyes. Take a deep breath in for 3 seconds, hold for 3 seconds, and as you exhale for 6 seconds, let go of any tension, stress, and the immortal identity. Allow yourself to settle into a state of calm and relaxation.

"I appreciate realizing that there is no cause and effect, for everything in this divine play of life is preordained. There is no need to force, resist, or manipulate anything. I surrender unconditionally to the Divine and stay Aware, witnessing this localized consciousness that perceives sensations, emotions, feelings, thoughts, imagination, and habitual tendencies of this body and mind known to me as [Your Name]. I remain aware, witnessing all impermanent transients in constant awareness. I remain the same constant and permanent Awareness from which 'I am' and all transients (functions of I Amness) rise, stay, and fall back to. I remain the same constant and permanent Awareness that witnessed the Big Bang, the birth of this Universe, and will see the end of time and space.

As I sit here in stillness, I become as innocent as a newborn, free from conditioning, limitations, beliefs, wants, needs, temptations, addictions, and identity. I remain absolutely formless, shapeless, birthless, deathless, timeless, and pure Awareness. I recognize that my body, without the mind, relies on innate intelligence. Even if I had amnesia, my body would wake up tomorrow and remain surrendered to this innate intelligence, regardless of my name or identity.

I observe my thoughts and emotions as they arise, understanding that they are transient and do not define my true essence. I let them pass without attachment or judgment, remaining rooted in the constant awareness that is my True Self. In this state, I find peace, joy, and serenity, knowing that I am connected to the infinite Awareness that transcends all forms and experiences.

Thank you, God, for helping me remain constant and grounded in my own awareness, observing all the transients that pass before me. I am grateful for the clarity and insight that come from recognizing my True Self, and I embrace the tranquility that accompanies this realization."

Take a few moments to sit in silence, breathing with purpose absorbing the peace and stillness of this meditation. When you are ready, gently open your eyes and bring your awareness back to the present moment, carrying a sense of calm and clarity with you throughout your day.

After 30 minutes of meditation, ask the Universe your questions and immediately write down the answers below:

Daily meditation routine before you go to bed or for best results create and listen to an audio or audible while falling asleep:

Meditation for Realizing the True-Self

Create a Sacred Space:

Find a quiet and peaceful place where you won't be disturbed.

Set a comfortable seating arrangement, perhaps with a cushion or chair, ensuring your spine is straight. Stretch before sitting down.

Begin with Deep Breathing:

Close your eyes and take several deep, calming breaths.

Inhale deeply through your nose for three seconds (inhale calmness and peace), hold for three seconds (hold the True Self), then exhale slowly through your mouth for six seconds (the primal mortal self).

Grounding Your Body:

As you breathe, become aware of your body. Feel the ground beneath you and how your body connects with it. Release any tension with each exhale, letting go of physical sensations and focusing on the stillness within.

Emptying the Mind:

Notice your emotions and thoughts without engaging with them. Imagine them as clouds passing by in the sky. Gently bring your focus back to your breath whenever your mind starts to wander. Your attention has great power, remind yourself of the transitory nature of thoughts and emotions and let them go.

Connecting with Pure Awareness:

Visualize yourself shedding layers of thoughts, emotions, memories, and primal identity. See these layers dissolving into the air around you. What remains is your pure awareness, the silent witness observing your experiences.

Deepening the Connection:

Rest in pure awareness and observe. Recognize this awareness connects all beings to a universal consciousness. Stay aware of the absence of contrast, experience, and transience.

Maintaining the Awareness:

As you sit, merge with a state of pure being. Notice the peace, clarity, and unity. Stay in Awareness for at least 30 minutes per session.

Gradual Return:

Slowly begin to bring your awareness back to your body and surroundings, while maintaining the sense of pure awareness. Take a few deep breaths, stretch gently, and open your eyes.

Tips for Practice:

Consistency: Practice this meditation daily, ideally at the same time, to build a strong connection with your True-Self.

Journaling:

Keep a journal to document your experiences and insights after each session.

Mindfulness:

Throughout the day, remind yourself of this state of pure awareness and try to carry it with you in your daily activities. Always remind yourself and identify as permanent Awareness and let go of all transients knowing that everything reflects the projection of One Awareness perceived through the lens of conditioning.

This practice can help you transcend the superficial layers of identity and align with the deep, peaceful essence of True-Self. Enjoy the journey of realizing and experiencing your highest true self in natural state of being.

References

1 Thanh Min, 2017. https://medium.com/motivationapp/the-elephant-rope-c22ee790a226

2 ZeroPark30,' The Story of Truth & Lie'. https://medium.com/@ParkerSimpson/the-story-of-truth-lie1476bda2d45e

3   https://home.cern/science/physics/higgs-boson

4 https://www.livescience.com/higgs-boson-particle

5 https://scienceexchange.caltech.edu/topics/quantum-science-explained/entanglement

6 https://www.worldhistory.org/Siddhartha_Gautama/

7 https://www.accesstoinsight.org/tipitaka/sn/sn56/sn56.011.than.html

8   https://www.accesstoinsight.org/tipitaka/sn/sn45/sn45.008.than.html

9 https://www.biblegateway.com/passage/?search=Matthew%204%3A1-11&version=NIV

10 https://www.biblegateway.com/passage/?search=Matthew%205-7&version=NIV

11 https://thepilgrim.co/cave-of-hira/

12 https://quran.com/en/al-alaq/1-5

13   https://thepilgrim.co/bani-shaiba/

14 https://quran.com/en/al-maidah/8

15 https://www.biblegateway.com/passage/?search=Exodus%202%3A11-15&version=NIV

16   https://www.biblegateway.com/passage/?search=Exodus%203%3A1-15&version=NIV

17   https://www.biblegateway.com/passage/?search=Exodus%2014%3A21-31&version=NIV

18 https://www.biblegateway.com/passage/?search=Numbers%2020%3A712&version=NIV

19 https://www.goodreads.com/book/show/30186948-think-and-grow-rich

20   https://www.listennotes.com/podcasts/prosperity-practice/a-parable-by-wayne-dyer-keyscPeE1VrBqsU/#google_vignette

21   https://www.ncbi.nlm.nih.gov/books/NBK92798/

22   https://my.clevelandclinic.org/health/articles/22839-glutamate

23   https://www.healthline.com/health/mental-health/serotonin

24   https://www.webmd.com/mental-health/what-isdopamine#:~:text=Dopamine%20is%20a%20complex%20hormone,like%20Parkinson's%2 0disease%20and%20schizophrenia.

25https://www.medicinenet.com/endorphins_natural_pain_and_stress_fighters/views.htm#: ~:text=Endorphins%20are%20among%20the%20brain, signals%20within%20the%20nervo us%20system.

26   https://my.clevelandclinic.org/health/articles/22610-norepinephrinenoradrenaline#:~:text=Norepinephrine%20(Noradrenaline)-,Norepinephrine%20(Noradrenaline),short%2Dterm%20serious%20health%2 0situations.

27 https://www.nasa.gov/image-article/einsteins-theory-of-relativity-critical-gps-seendistant-stars/

28 https://www.space.com/17661-theory-general-relativity.html

29https://catalogofbias.org/biases/perceptionbias/#:~:text=Perception%20bias%20is%20the%20tendency,influenced%20by%20percepti on%20biases%20unconsciously.

30https://www.researchgate.net/publication/233556531_The_Science_of_Art _A_Neurologica l_Theory_of_Aesthetic_Experience

31   http://cogweb.ucla.edu/ep/EP-primer.html

32 https://www.healthline.com/health/what-is-change-blindness-and-why-does-it-happen

33   https://plato.stanford.edu/entries/spinoza/#Biog

34   https://open.bu.edu/handle/2144/9201

35 https://www.prospectmagazine.co.uk/culture/37996/spinozas-god-einstein-believed-in-it-but-what-was-it

36 https://www.podiumsportsjournal.com/2010/10/01/how-to-achieve-the-flow-state-inathletics-and-life/#:~:text=%E2%80%9CFlow%E2%80%9D%20is%20a%20state%20of,perform%20at %20extremely%20high%20levels.

36   https://futurism.com/sir-roger-penrose-alternate-theory-of-the-big-bang-2

37 Arsen, D. S. (2020, November 19). Is Karma Real? Is Karma What You Think? Are Your Health and Wellness Affected by Karma? Can you Plant Positive Karma Seeds And Change Your Life!: Dr. Sarah Larsen ~ Medical Intuitive and Energy Healer. Retrieved from https://drsarahlarsen.com/is-karma-real-is-karma-what-you-think-is-your-health-andwellness-affected-by-karma-can-you-plant-positive-karma-seeds-and-change-your-life/

38 August 23, 2. (2017, August 23). The Leading Edge. Retrieved from https://edge.oregonstate.edu/2017/08/23/the-science-of-karma/

39 Siegel, E. (2019, March 15). This Is Why The Multiverse Must Exist. Retrieved from https://www.forbes.com/sites/startswithabang/2019/03/15/this-is-why-the-multiverse-mustexist/?sh=18ee61556d08

40 https://theselfhelplibrary.com/the-power-of-service-finding-yourself-through-helpingothers/

41 https://themaddphilosopher.com/2015/06/02/the-three-virtues-of-service-more-than-justdoing-what-you-love/

42 https://themaddphilosopher.com/2015/06/02/the-three-virtues-of-service-more-than-justdoing-what-you-love/